HAL LEONARD

CHINESE PIPA METHOD

BY GAO HONG

To access video, visit:
www.halleonard.com/mylibrary

Enter Code
3859-8067-7156-4635

ISBN 978-1-4803-5239-1

HAL•LEONARD®
CORPORATION

7777 W. BLUEMOUND RD. P.O. BOX 13819 MILWAUKEE, WI 53213

In Australia Contact:
Hal Leonard Australia Pty. Ltd.
4 Lentara Court
Cheltenham, Victoria, 3192 Australia
Email: ausadmin@halleonard.com.au

Visit Hal Leonard Online at
www.halleonard.com

CONTENTS

	PAGE	VIDEO LESSON
INTRODUCTION	4	
HOW TO USE THIS BOOK	4	
About the Video Examples	4	
ABOUT THE AUTHOR	5	
ACKNOWLEDGMENTS	5	
ABOUT THE PIPA	6	
Parts of the Pipa	6	
String and Peg Positions	7	
Fingerpicks on the Right Hand	7	
Holding the Pipa	8	
Taking Care of Your Pipa	8	
CHINESE NOTATION	9	
Example: Jingle Bells	11	
RANGES OF THE PIPA: OPEN STRINGS	12	
Standard Open-String Tuning	12	
TAN AND TIAO	14	1–4
OPEN-STRING CROSSING	16	
String-Crossing Exercises	16	5
THE KEY OF D	17	6
PIPA POSITIONS	18	
LEFT-HAND SYMBOLS AND TECHNIQUES	19	
Pressing the String	20	
THE FIRST POSITION (I)	21	7–14
Shuang Tan, Shuang Tiao, Sao, Fo, Zhe, and Fen	23	15–18
THE SECOND POSITION (II)	26	19–20
Happy Yi People	28	21
XIANG (0) AND THIRD (III) POSITIONS	29	22–23
Little Bok Choy	31	24
POSITION CHANGES	32	
Position Changes Part I	32	25–28
Position Changes Part II	33	29–32
TREMOLO / LUN ZHI	36	
San Zhi Lun	36	33–34
Si Zhi Lun / Ban Lun	37	35–36
Combining Techniques	39	
Golden Snake Dance	40	37–38
Wu Zhi Lun / Five-Finger Tremolo	42	39–44
Chang Lun Five-Finger Long Tremolo and Gun Zhi	45	45–46
Colored Clouds Chasing the Moon (Excerpt)	46	47–48

	PAGE	VIDEO LESSON

NOTE BENDING 47

    Tui 47 49–50

    La/Wan 48

    Flying Kites 48 51

VIBRATO AND OVERTONES 50

    Yin 50 52

    Rou 50

    Jasmine Flower 50 53

    Fanyin (Overtones) 51

    Three Variations of Plum Blossoms 53 54

THE KEY OF C 54 55

    Drum Song from Fengyang 56 56–57

THE KEY OF G 59 58

    Selling Rice Balls 62 59

RIGHT-HAND SOUND EFFECT TECHNIQUES 64

    Arpeggios / Gua and Lin 64

    Flying Song 64 60–61

    Zhai, Pai, Ti, and Tan Mianban Techniques 67 62

    Yi Folk Tune 68 63

LEFT-HAND SPECIAL TECHNIQUES 69

    Da, Sou, and Dai 69

    Chanting 70 64–66

MORE SPECIAL TECHNIQUES 73

    Jiao, Sha, and Fu 73 67–68

    Celebration 73 69–71

CHINESE SILK AND BAMBOO MUSIC 76

    Jiangnan Sizhu 76

    Purple Bamboo 78 72–73

    Guangdong Yinyue 80

    Thunder in a Dry Season 80 74–76

CLASSICAL PIPA REPERTOIRE 83

    White Snow in Sunny Spring (Yang Chun Bai Xue) 84 77–91

APPENDIX 100

    Composing for Pipa 100

    Pipa Sound Effects 101 92

    String Symbols 102

    Left-Hand Fingering Symbols 102

    Left-Hand Position Symbols 102

    Left-Hand Techniques 102

    Right-Hand Techniques 103

INTRODUCTION

The *Hal Leonard Chinese Pipa Method* provides an introduction for English speakers on how to play the basic techniques on the pipa. No previous experience is necessary, and the book is suitable for all ages. It is ideal for use in three different areas:

1. For anyone interested in learning how to play the Chinese pipa;

2. For guitar or lute players who would like to adapt pipa techniques to their own instruments;

3. For composers who want to learn how to use pipa techniques and notate scores for their own compositions.

This book includes both Western and Chinese simplified notation for each score for easy reference and comparison. It uses popular folk tunes from different regions and ethnic groups as exercise pieces. This makes it possible to learn new techniques while learning how to play Chinese traditional music. Since this book is targeted for self-taught English-speakers, it focuses primarily on the easiest and most common key to start with—the key of D. To broaden the content, there are also brief introductions to the keys of C and G. Throughout the entire book you will see valuable information and examples of left-hand and right-hand techniques and positions that can be used as references when composing for pipa or for adapting pipa techniques to your own instruments. A bonus video also provides a summary of special sound effects for composers.

HOW TO USE THIS BOOK

There are ten total levels in Chinese pipa training. This step-by-step method book includes instruction equivalent to levels 1 through 4, which focus on basic right- and left-hand techniques in the key of D. Levels 5–10 focus on a variety of repertoire from classical, traditional, and modern compositions in a variety of keys. For best results, follow each step in the order they appear. This will assure you acquire good playing habits. For each technique, take as much time as needed to learn it. Do not move on to the next step until you are comfortable with the previous one and you can execute it naturally. Avoid rushing from step to step.

ABOUT THE VIDEO EXAMPLES

 All of the accompanying videos for this book can be accessed online for streaming or download. Simply visit **www.halleonard.com/mylibrary** and enter the code found on page 1 of this book. Video examples are noted throughout the book with the icon seen here.

Most examples include two videos showing proper techniques for both hands where applicable. It is best to start each step by watching the video to get an idea of what you are trying to accomplish. Then you can play along with the video or practice the technique yourself. Also, read the texts carefully for each lesson before you begin to play. Here is an example of how to proceed with each lesson:

1. Read the texts showing you how to play the techniques.

2. Watch the video for each lesson before you play.

3. Follow the instructions and try it yourself.

4. It helps to look into a mirror while playing to assure your hand positions are correct.

5. Read all the notes included with the exercises. The notes offer helpful hints and other options.

6. Be patient! Do not rush to the next exercise until you are comfortable with the previous one.

7. Have fun!

ABOUT THE AUTHOR

Gao Hong, a Chinese musical prodigy and master of the pipa, began her career as a professional musician at age 12. She graduated with honors from China's premier music school, the Central Conservatory of Music in Beijing, where she studied with the great pipa master Lin Shicheng. In both China and the U.S., as a performer, composer, and educator, Gao has received awards and honors too numerous to list. She has performed throughout Europe, Australia, Japan, Hong Kong, China, and the U.S. in solo concerts and with symphony orchestras, jazz musicians, choirs, and musicians from various other cultures. She is currently on the music faculty of Carleton College, where she teaches Chinese instruments and directs the Chinese Music Ensemble. She is also a guest professor at the Central Conservatory of Music in Beijing and on the faculty of Macalester College and McNally Smith College of Music in St. Paul. Visit **www.chinesepipa.com** to find out about her numerous music releases, performance schedule, and remarkable life journey.

ACKNOWLEDGMENTS

English Editors: Greg Herriges, Paul Dice
Chinese Paintings: Yang Lan
Photography: Bob Otsuka
Video: Maximiliano Villarreal, Xiaodi Wang

My heartfelt thanks go out to Hal Leonard Corporation for their willingness to promote Chinese traditional music in America.

A big thank you for the unconditional support of Carleton College, my colleagues, and my students:

Steven Richardson, Puzak Family Director of the Arts – Office of the Director of Arts
Dann Hurlbert, Media & Design Specialist – PEPS Presentation, Events & Production Support
Paul Bernhardt, Audio and Visual Technical Director – Cinema and Media Studies
Department of Music, and 182, 282, and 188 courses' students

Many thanks to Greg Herriges, Bob Otsuka, Maximiliano Villarreal, and Xiaodi Wang for their hard work and dedication.

A big thank you to my lovely family in China, my sweet husband Paul Dice, and my beautiful daughter Alida for their unconditional love and support.

Thanks for the outstanding support of the Minnesota State Arts Board Folk and Traditional Arts Grant for making this wonderful project possible. *This activity is made possible in part by a grant provided by the Minnesota State Arts Board through an appropriation by the Minnesota State Legislature from the State's arts and cultural heritage fund with money from the vote of the people of Minnesota on November 4, 2008.*

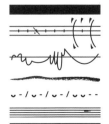

CLEAN WATER LAND & LEGACY AMENDMENT

MINNESOTA STATE ARTS BOARD

ABOUT THE PIPA

The **pipa** is a pear-shaped, plucked, stringed instrument with four strings and 30 (or 31) frets. The word "pipa" is made up of two Chinese characters: 琵 ("pi") and 琶 ("pa").

PARTS OF THE PIPA

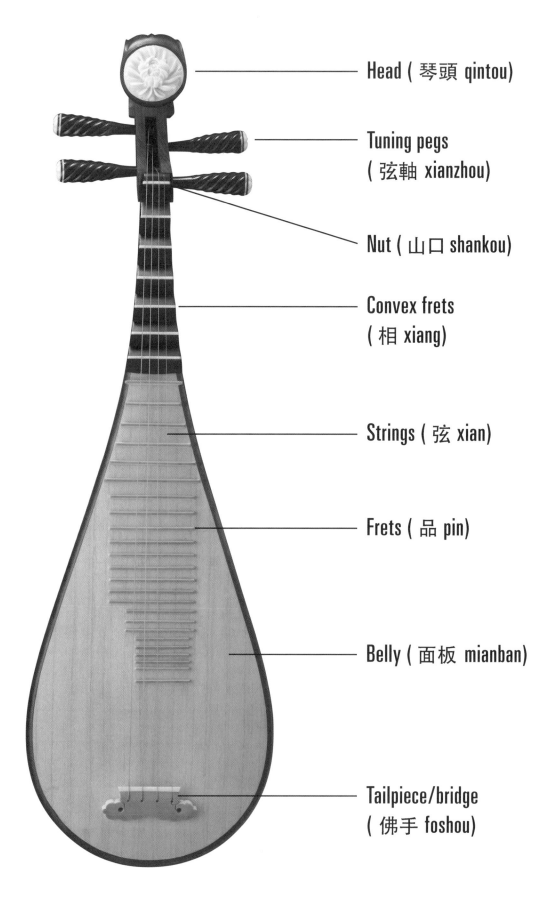

Head (琴頭 qintou)

Tuning pegs
(弦軸 xianzhou)

Nut (山口 shankou)

Convex frets
(相 xiang)

Strings (弦 xian)

Frets (品 pin)

Belly (面板 mianban)

Tailpiece/bridge
(佛手 foshou)

STRING AND PEG POSITIONS

The pipa has four strings. The thinnest string with the highest pitch is the first string. The thickest string is the fourth string and it has the lowest pitch.

The first and third strings are tied to the pegs on the right side as you are facing the pipa. The second and fourth strings are tied to the pegs on the left side.

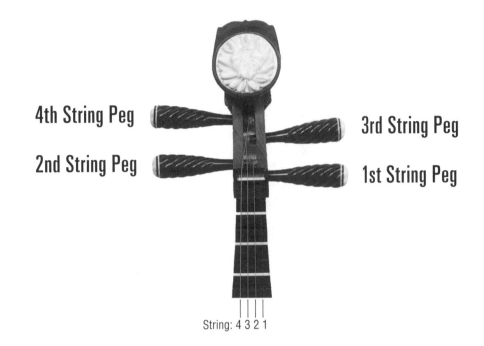

4th String Peg

2nd String Peg

3rd String Peg

1st String Peg

String: 4 3 2 1

FINGERPICKS ON THE RIGHT HAND

The player wears fingerpicks made of bone, shell, or a special type of nylon, which are bound by surgical tape over the fingernails. The fingerpicks are placed on top of the player's nails and should not extend more than 2 to 3 mm (about 1/10") beyond the end of the fingernails. The surgical tape should be placed over the bottom 1/3 of each fingerpick. Make sure the tape is not too tight or too loose.

Correct Placement of the Surgical Tape

Turtle Shell Fingerpicks

7

HOLDING THE PIPA

The way you hold the pipa is very different from the way you hold a guitar, as shown:

- Select a knee-high, armless chair or stool.

- Hold the pipa upright, rest it on your thighs, and tilt it slightly to the left.

- Shoulders should be in a natural and relaxed position.

- Sit slightly forward in the chair.

TAKING CARE OF YOUR PIPA

After playing, put the pipa back in its case or bag. To avoid getting cracks in the body, do not put the pipa in direct sunlight or close to a heating vent or any other heat source.

CHINESE NOTATION

Most traditional pipa scores today are written in a Chinese cipher notation system called **Jianpu**—a simplified numerical notation system which corresponds to Western *solfege: do*=1, *re*=2, *mi*=3, etc.

C Major

Notation:	1	2	3	4	5	6	7
Solfege:	do	re	mi	fa	sol	la	ti
Note:	C	D	E	F	G	A	B

A dot above the note indicates an octave higher:

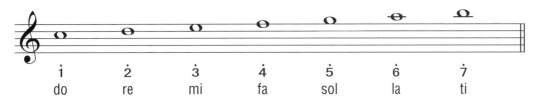

1	2	3	4	5	6	7
do	re	mi	fa	sol	la	ti

A dot below the note indicates an octave lower:

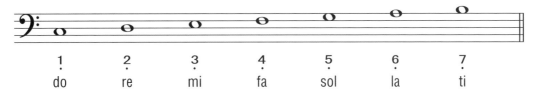

1	2	3	4	5	6	7
do	re	mi	fa	sol	la	ti

If the note is more than an octave higher or lower, more dots are added above or below:

Key changes are marked in the upper left-hand corner at the beginning of the piece in the following manner: 1=D for the key of D, 1=G for the key of G, and so on.

D Major (1=D)

Notation:	1	2	3	4	5	6	7
Solfege:	do	re	mi	fa	sol	la	ti
Note:	D	E	F♯	G	A	B	C♯

G Major (1=G)

Notation:	1	2	3	4	5	6	7
Solfege:	do	re	mi	fa	sol	la	ti
Note:	G	A	B	C	D	E	F♯

Dashes, lines, and dots are placed after or below the notes to indicate note values. It is somewhat similar to Western notation. While a number alone represents a note of one beat, a dash represents one beat of duration for a held note.

Lines below the note name indicate eighths, sixteenths, etc. A dotted note lasts for one and a half beats.

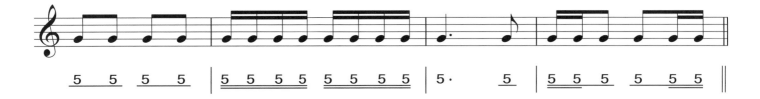

Rests are indicated by the number "0," with corresponding lines, dots, and repeats.

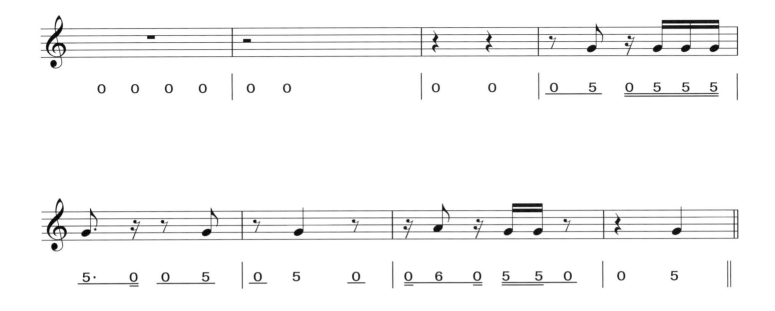

EXAMPLE: JINGLE BELLS

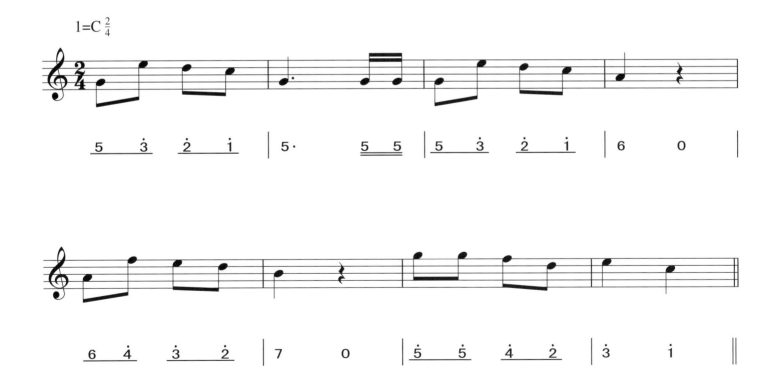

RANGES OF THE PIPA: OPEN STRINGS

The pipa has four ranges of notes, spanning many octaves and tone colors.

Four Ranges of the Pipa

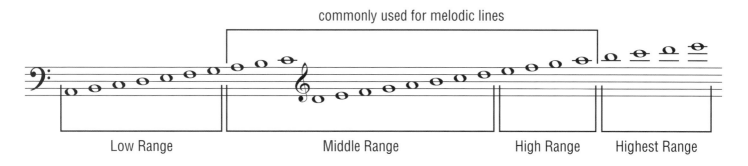

Common Usage and Characteristics of the Four Ranges:

1. **Low Range** – solid, forceful, and dark tone color; used to add a special color to the melody or chords.

2. **Middle Range** – mild, gentle, pure, and sweet tone color; commonly used for melodic lines.

3. **High Range** – melodious, clear, and shining tone color; commonly used for melodic lines.

4. **Highest Range** – sharp, tense, and bright tone color; used to add tension, emotion, or excitement to the melody. This range is not used very often; it is used primarily at climactic moments.

The middle range and high range provide the best sound quality on pipa. Therefore, many pieces are written in these ranges. These are also the most comfortable positions to play in.

STANDARD OPEN-STRING TUNING

Within this standard tuning, the *Jianpu* cipher notation system is similar to the moveable solfege system. Therefore, as the keys change, the tuning of the strings remains intact (A–D–E–A), but the solfege and cipher notation numbers change. For example, in the key of C, the note A would be "la" or "6," while in the key of D, it would be "sol" or "5." Here are some examples:

Standard Open-String Tuning (A–D–E–A)	Cipher Notation/Solfege	
1=C	(6 2 3 6)	la re mi la
1=D	(5 1 2 5)	sol do re sol
1=G	(2 5 6 2)	re sol la re
1=F	(3 6 7 3)	mi la ti mi
1=A	(1 4 5 1)	do fa sol do

Symbols specifying which string to play on are written below the numbers in the notation.

To indicate open strings, parentheses ( ) are added as shown:

(x) 4th open string   (三) 3rd open string   (II) 2nd open string   (—) 1st open string

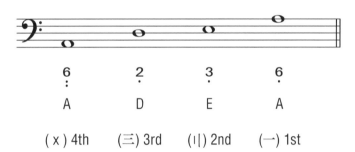

6	2	3	6
A	D	E	A
(x) 4th	(三) 3rd	(II) 2nd	(—) 1st

ALTERNATE TUNINGS

There are only a few traditional pieces in pipa repertoire that use alternate tunings. In the early 20th century, several composers started experimenting with alternate tunings such as A–B–E–A and G–D–E–A. In 1991, world-renowned Chinese-American composer Chen Yi's solo pipa composition "The Points" was the first to feature the dissonant open tuning B♭–D♯–E–A that included both flat and sharp open-string notes.

TAN AND TIAO

Tan and **Tiao** (彈 和 挑) are the primary right-hand playing techniques. Almost all other right-hand techniques are based on *Tan* and *Tiao*, so it is very important to learn these techniques correctly.

The right-hand playing techniques are indicated by symbols placed above the numbers.

　　╲ **Tan:** The right-hand index finger plucks the string with a downward motion.

　　╱ **Tiao:** The right-hand thumb plucks the string with an upward motion.

Tan and Tiao on the First Open String

Open-String Tuning 1=C (6 2 3 6)

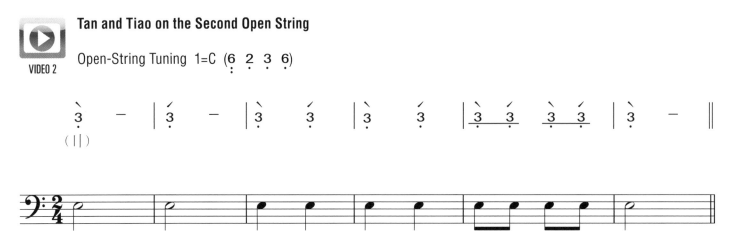

To avoid touching other strings when playing on the second, third, and fourth strings, quickly retract your finger and thumb after plucking. The overall motion is less than when plucking the first string. This applies to the third and fourth strings as well.

Tan and Tiao on the Second Open String

Open-String Tuning 1=C (6 2 3 6)

Tan and Tiao on the Third Open String

Open-String Tuning 1=C (6̣ 2̇ 3̇ 6̣)

Tan and Tiao on the Fourth Open String

Open-String Tuning 1=C (6̣ 2̇ 3̇ 6̣)

OPEN-STRING CROSSING

STRING-CROSSING EXERCISES

When crossing strings, the best plucking position differs with each string. Here is a guide indicating the best plucking position for each string:

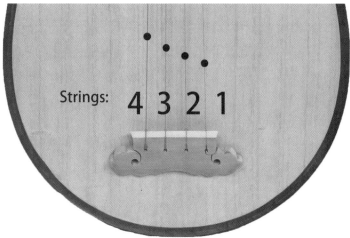

When practicing, start out at a slow tempo and slowly increase speed as your fingers become more flexible. Keep your hand in a natural, relaxed position at all times.

Open-String Crossing in the Key of C

VIDEO 5   Open-String Tuning 1=C (6 2 3 6)

THE KEY OF D

The key of D is the most common key found in pipa music. Therefore, it is the first key in which you will learn left-hand techniques. In the key of D, the open strings are: (5̣ 1̣ 2̣ 5̣)

▶ Open-String Crossing in the Key of D

VIDEO 6

Open-String Tuning 1=D (5̣ 1̣ 2̣ 5̣)

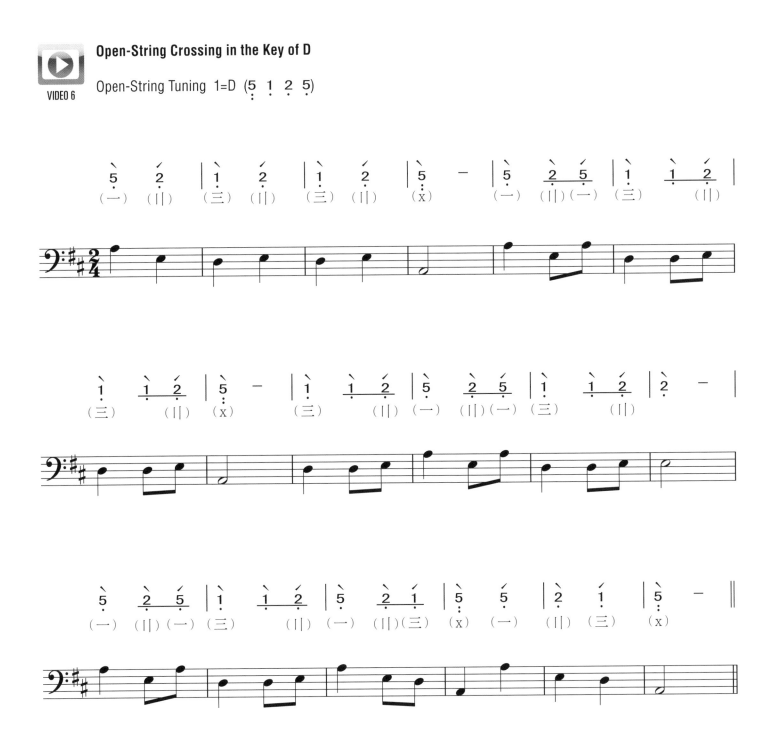

Focus on reading Chinese notation and familiarizing yourself with *Tan* and *Tiao* techniques until you are comfortable and ready for the next lesson. It's important to master *Tan* and *Tiao* before moving on to learning left-hand techniques.

PIPA POSITIONS

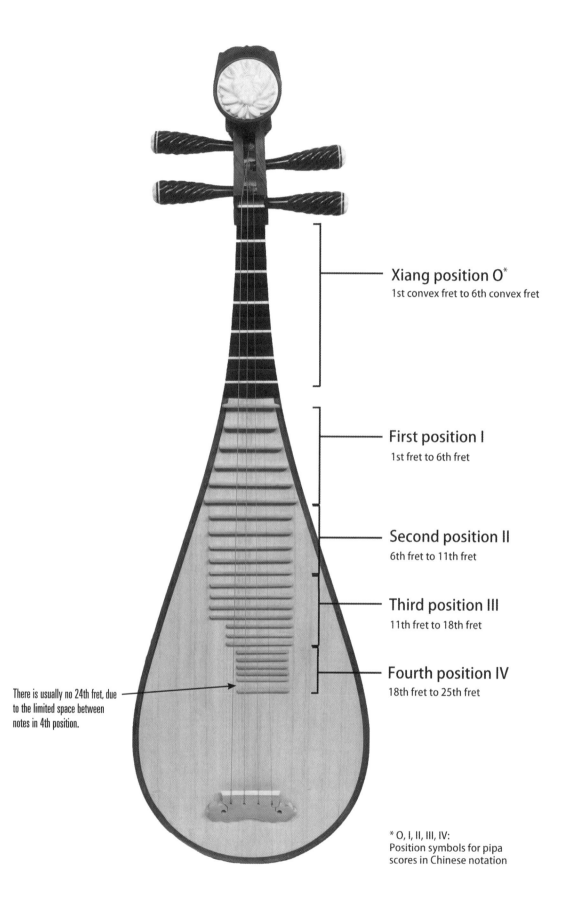

Xiang position O*
1st convex fret to 6th convex fret

First position I
1st fret to 6th fret

Second position II
6th fret to 11th fret

Third position III
11th fret to 18th fret

There is usually no 24th fret, due to the limited space between notes in 4th position.

Fourth position IV
18th fret to 25th fret

* O, I, II, III, IV:
Position symbols for pipa scores in Chinese notation

LEFT-HAND SYMBOLS AND TECHNIQUES

Left-Hand Symbols in Western and Chinese Notation

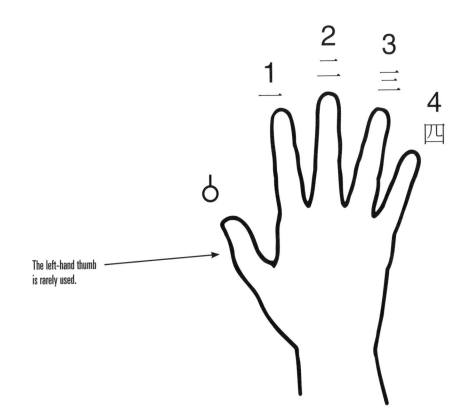

The left-hand thumb is rarely used.

Left-hand symbols are placed to the left of the numbers.

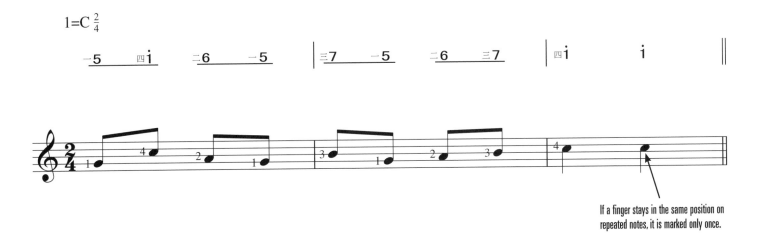

If a finger stays in the same position on repeated notes, it is marked only once.

PRESSING THE STRING

When pressing the string on the frets, bend knuckles naturally. They should be curved and not stiff. Use only your fingertips to press the string.

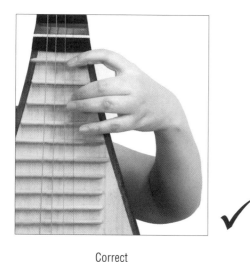

Correct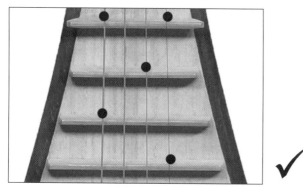

Incorrect

The left-hand thumb should rest comfortably on the back of the pipa.

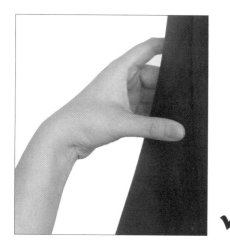

Correct

Incorrect

The thumb should be directly behind the middle finger or between the middle and index fingers for the first position. For higher positions it is placed behind the index finger or between the the middle and index fingers. It should not be pressed too tightly against the pipa. This applies to all positions except the fourth position, where it is necessary to bring the thumb to the front of the pipa.

Placement of the Fingertips

When pressing the string, correct placement of the fingertip is very important. The string should be pressed very close to the fret, but not over or on the fret, nor in the middle between the two frets.

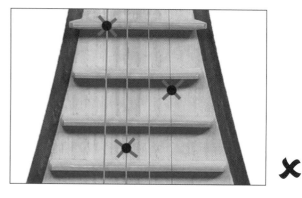

Correct

Incorrect

THE FIRST POSITION (I)

Key of D: First Position (I) 1=D

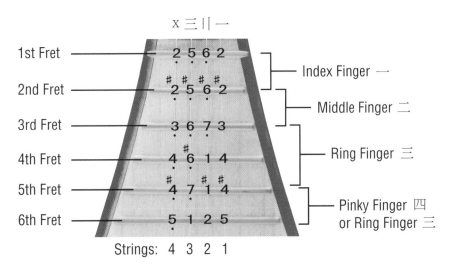

1st Fret — 2 5 6 2 — Index Finger 一
2nd Fret — #2 #5 #6 #2 — Middle Finger 二
3rd Fret — 3 6 7 3 — Ring Finger 三
4th Fret — 4 #6 1 4 —
5th Fret — #4 7 1 #4 — Pinky Finger 四 or Ring Finger 三
6th Fret — 5 1 2 5 —

Strings: 4 3 2 1

The pinky is the weakest finger of all. In the beginning, you may have trouble producing a clear sound with this finger. This is very normal for beginners. To make a clear sound, use the tip of the pinky and relax all the other fingers while pressing the string.

VIDEOS 7–8
(left hand/right hand)

Key of D First Position (I) on the First and Second Strings

Open-String Tuning 1=D (5 1 2 5)

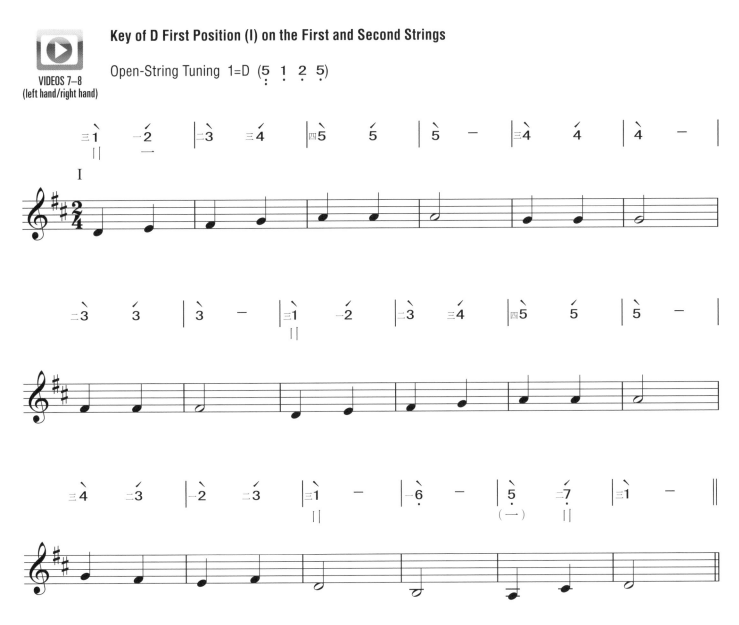

After playing a note, the left-hand fingers should not be lifted too far away from the string. Fingers need to be kept in a relaxed position. Use your fingertips and do not flatten your fingers.

Key of D First Position (I) on the Third and Fourth Strings

Open-String Tuning 1=D (5 1 2 5)

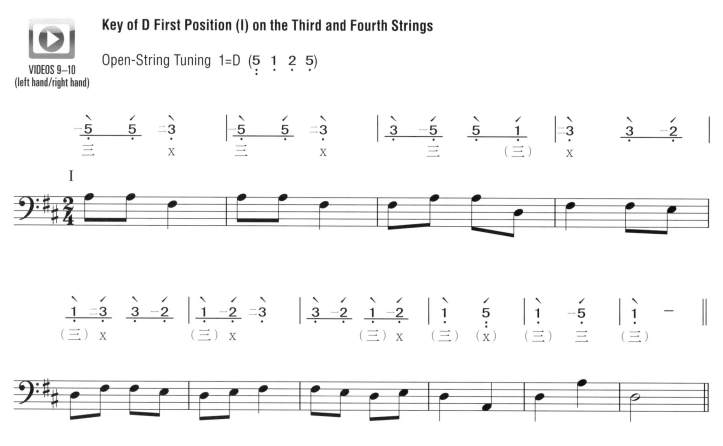

Scale exercises are very important. Here is one that covers the key of D on all four strings. Start at a slow pace. Try to memorize all the finger positions for each note. This will help you greatly in learning the first position on your left hand.

First Position (I) Key of D Scale

Open-String Tuning 1=D (5 1 2 5)

After pressing a note, prepare immediately to move the next finger into position. Do not lift your finger too high; keep it close to the position of the next note. Practice this slowly at first until you are comfortable enough to speed up.

The thumb should be placed lightly on the back of the pipa and should remain stationary as you move your fingers to play different notes.

Key of D First Position (I) Combining All Four Strings

Open-String Tuning 1=D (5 1 2 5)

SHUANG TAN, SHUANG TIAO, SAO, FO, ZHE, AND FEN

Shuang Tan 雙彈 (╲): In Chinese, *Shuang* means "double." *Shuang Tan* means double *Tan*. The right-hand index finger plucks with a downward motion on two strings.

Shuang Tiao 雙挑(∥): *Shuang Tiao* means "double *Tiao*." The right-hand thumb plucks with an upward motion on two strings.

Sao 掃 (➘): The right-hand index finger strikes with a downward motion on four strings.

Fo 佛 (➚): The right-hand thumb strikes with an upward motion on four strings.

When using these four techniques, your right-hand thumb and index finger can be pressed together for better control. When using the *Sao* and *Fo* techniques, your arm and wrist can swing up and down to assist your fingers and add impact.

Key of D First Position (I) Shuang Tan, Shuang Tiao and Sao, Fo Exercise

Open-String Tuning 1=D (5 1 2 5)

Uygur Folk Tune 維吾爾族民歌

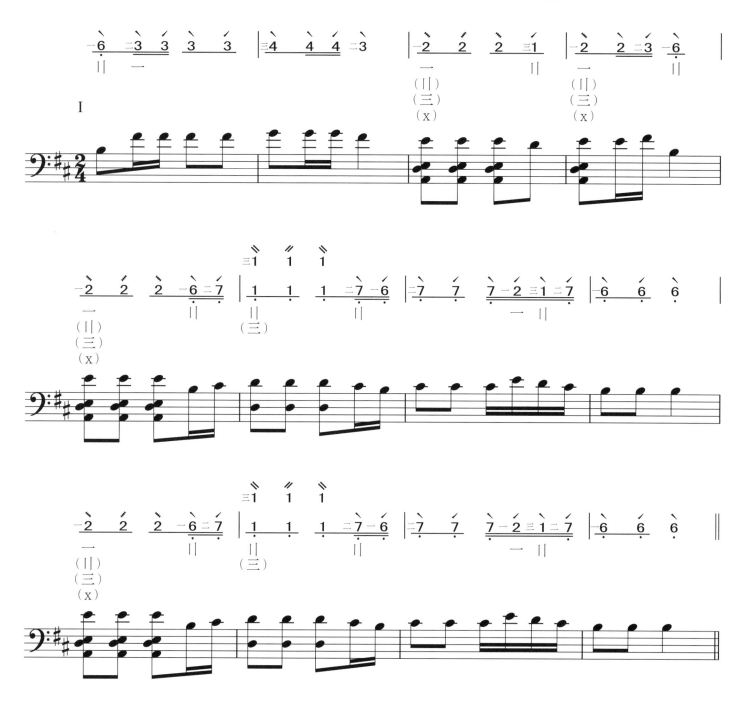

Zhe ⊂⊃ (摭): The right-hand index finger and thumb pluck two strings simultaneously with the fingernail tip and thumbnail tip moving towards each other.

Fen ⟋⟍ (分): The right-hand index finger snd thumb pluck two strings simultaneously with the fingernail tip and thumbnail tip moving in opposite directions.

VIDEOS 17–18
(left hand/right hand)

Key of D First Position (I) Zhe, Fen and Sao, Fo Exercise

Open-String Tuning 1=D (5 1 2 5)

Dai Folk Tune 傣族民歌

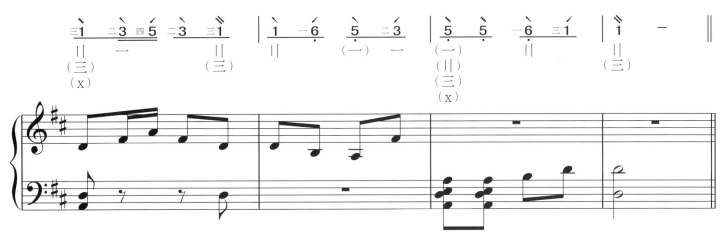

In the techniques you just learned—*Shuang Tan*, *Shuang Tiao*, *Sao*, *Fo*, *Zhe*, and *Fen*—two or four strings are sounded together to produce a harmony or double the volume. Make sure they are played simultaneously and not separately.

THE SECOND POSITION (II)

Key of D Second Position (II) 1=D

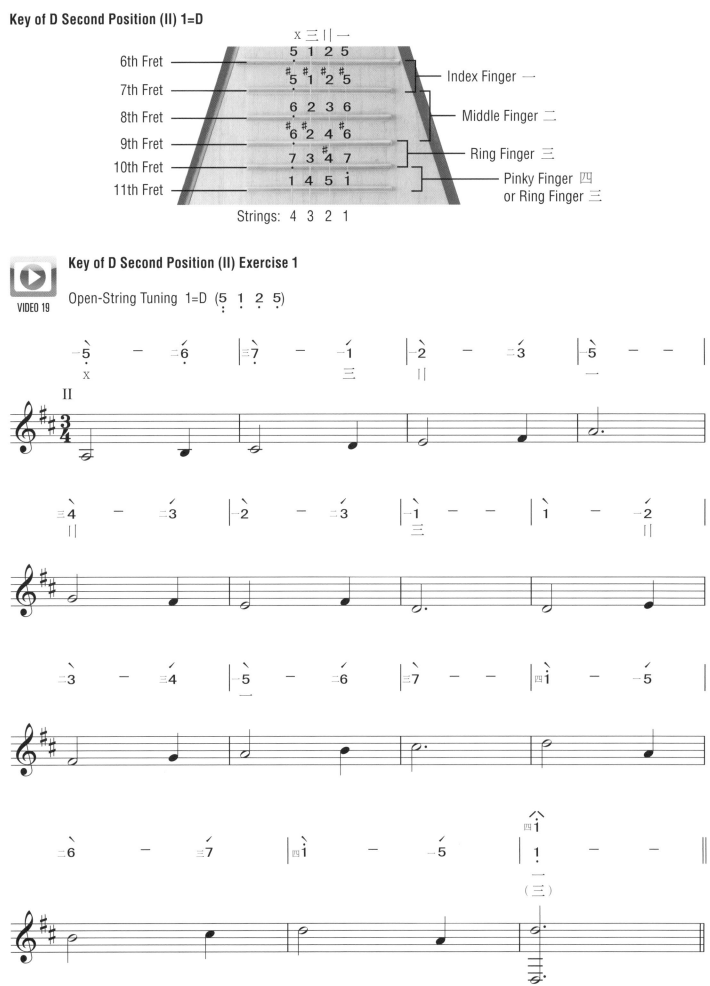

Key of D Second Position (II) Exercise 1

VIDEO 19

Open-String Tuning 1=D (5̣ 1̣ 2̣ 5̣)

VIDEO 20

Key of D Second Position (II) Exercise 2

It's very important to keep your left-hand adjacent finger on the string when using other fingers to play higher notes on the same string.

When two *Tan* techniques occur next to each other, the first *Tan* is always louder than the second one.

Open-String Tuning 1=D (5̣ 1 2 5̣)

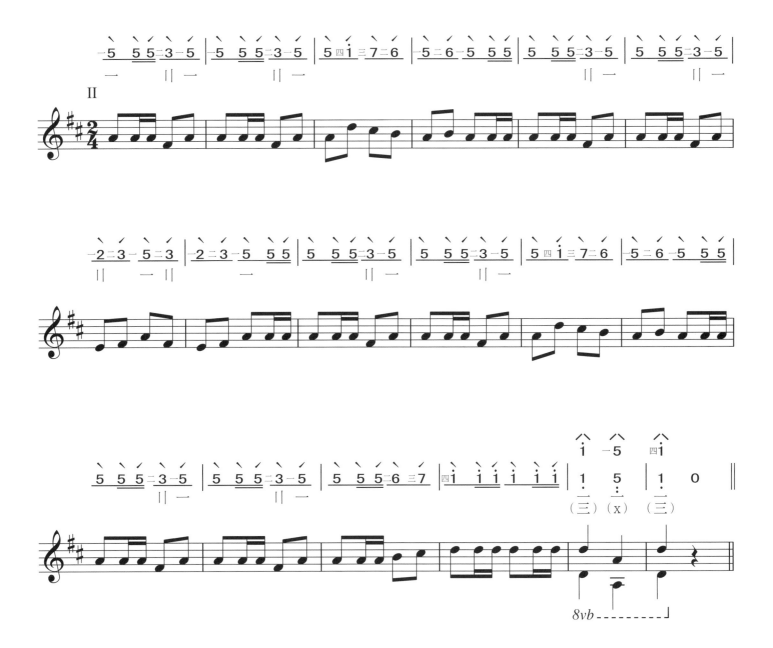

ETHNIC GROUPS IN CHINA

The People's Republic of China (PRC) has 1.3 billion people. China officially recognizes 55 ethnic minority groups within China in addition to the Han majority. Each of the minority groups has its own distinct culture and customs. The Xizang Province (Tibet) and Xinjiang Province have more minority people than Han people. The Uygur people mainly live in the Xinjiang Uygur Autonomous Region in northwestern China. They practice Islam, and have their own music, dance, and customs. Yunnan Province has 21 minority groups, including Yi, Miao (Hmong), Yao, Dai, Bai, etc. They are versatile people who have many achievements in music—some of which are taught in this book. They practice Buddhism, Islam, Christianity, Taoism, Polytheism, and other religions.

When two notes using the same finger occur next to each other, you can flatten your finger to press on both strings simultaneously. This is the only time it's okay *not* to use your fingertip!

In "Happy Yi People," the "2" (re) can be played on either the second or third string—whichever is easier. This determination is made based on what note follows the "2."

Notice the repeats ‖: :‖ and first and second endings in this tune. The first repeat sign sends you back to the beginning. Repeat the first section once, then play through the second section. When you reach the first ending, go back to the previous repeat sign, then play through the rest of the tune with the second ending (skipping the first ending).

HAPPY YI PEOPLE
快樂的羅嗦

XIANG (0) AND THIRD (III) POSITIONS

The first and second positions are the most common positions due to the brighter sounds produced. Sometimes, however, the **Xiang** position (0), third position (III), and fourth position (IV) are used for special lower or higher sound effects.

Xiang Position (0)

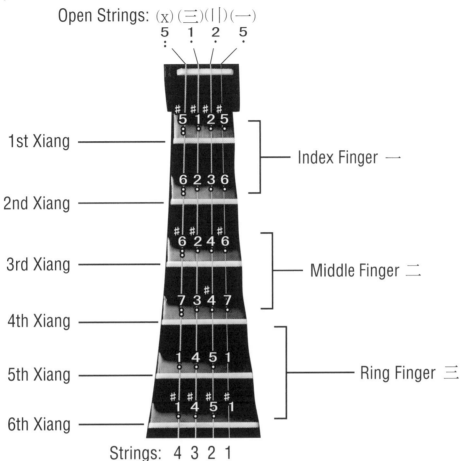

Correct   Incorrect

Many of the same notes playable in the *Xiang* position (0) can also be played in the first position on the second, third, and fourth strings. *Xiang* position (0) is only used when the composer or piece warrants a brighter sound or to make it easier when combining techniques such as *Zhe* ◯ or *Fen* ◢◣ .

VIDEOS 22–23
(left hand/right hand)

Xiang Position (0) Exercise

Open-String Tuning 1=D (5 1 2 5)

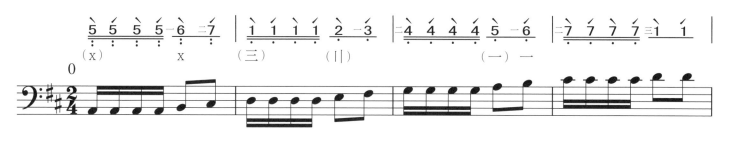

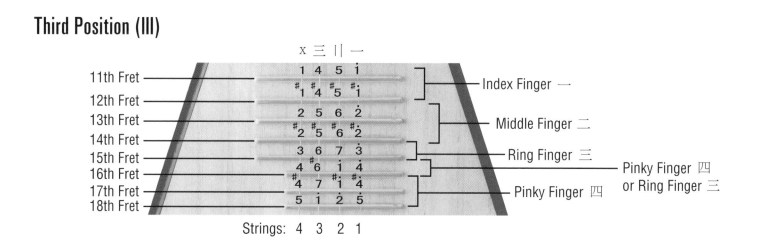

Third Position (III)

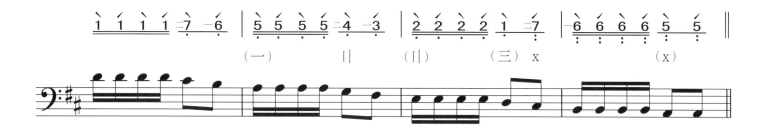

11th Fret
12th Fret
13th Fret
14th Fret
15th Fret
16th Fret
17th Fret
18th Fret

Strings: 4 3 2 1

In third position (III) the left-hand thumb is placed on the back of the pipa, and the third and fourth strings are rarely used due to the darker sound. The pinky should be used to play on both note 4 (fa) and 5 (sol).

"Little Bok Choy" is in the unusual **5/4** time signature with five beats per measure. The **ritard** *(rit.)* in the final measure indicates that the music slows down, ending with a **fermata** (⌢)—the final note is held and sustained beyond the duration of the measure.

LITTLE BOK CHOY

小白菜

♩ = 68   Open-String Tuning 1=D (5̣ 1̣ 2̣ 5̣)   Hebei Folk Tune   河北民歌

VIDEO 24

STORYTELLING IN PIPA MUSIC

There are three types of pipa storytelling music: **Wen**, **Wu**, and **Da**.

Wen style (文曲) is slower in tempo, and typically describes scenes of nature, and people's emotions. "Moonlight Over the Spring River" (春江花月夜) is a famous piece in *Wen* style.

Wu style (武曲) is generally more rhythmic, stronger and faster in tempo, and often depicts scenes in battles where the pipa imitates sound effects such as horses neighing, wind blowing, screaming people, swords clashing, and cannon shots. A famous piece in *Wu* style is "Ambush from All Sides" (十面埋伏).

Da style （大曲） is a combination of both of *Wen* and *Wu* styles. *Da*-style pieces usually contain multiple sections, and can describe both scenes of nature and imitate sound effects to depict events in a story. "Dragon Boat" (龍船) is a famous piece in *Da* style.

POSITION CHANGES

POSITION CHANGES PART I

Position changes are very common when playing a musical score. There are many ways to change positions. Here are the most common ways…

Using an Open String to Change Position

Using an open string to change positions is very convenient. While plucking the open string with your right hand, your left hand can simultaneously move to the next position.

VIDEOS 25–26
(left hand/right hand)

Open-String Tuning 1=D (5̣ 1̇ 2̇ 5̣)

Using the Same Finger to Change Positions

Using the same finger to change positions is very common. When you move from a lower position to a higher position (e.g., position I to position II), the left-hand thumb follows the wrist and arm to slide down first with your finger barely touching the string. When you reach the next position note, lift your wrist back into a natural position, keeping your fingers together. Don't let your finger leave the string during the transfer, but do not press on the frets or too hard on the string, as this would make extra unnecessary sounds.

When you move to the next lower position (e.g., from position II to position I), your left-hand thumb follows your wrist and arm in an upward motion first. Your finger should stay on the string, barely touching it until you reach the next position note. Your left-hand fingers should be kept together. Do not stiffen them—keep them relaxed. Do not leave the string during the transfer and do not jump to the next position. Do not press on the frets or press too hard on the string.

When two *Tan* techniques appear next to each other in a slow tempo, the second *Tan* will start just like the first one; your arm and wrist should follow your finger to make a natural circular motion. This type of slow *Tan* is commonly used in *Wen*-style pieces.

VIDEOS 27–28
(left hand/right hand)

POSITION CHANGES PART II

So far you have learned how to use open strings and the same finger to change positions. Now we will explore two other options: **using different fingers to change positions**, and **stretching a finger to change positions**.

The following example uses both techniques in a **pentatonic** (five-note) **scale** exercise. The techniques are shown in the notation with corresponding numbers:

① Using Different Fingers to Change Positions

② Stretching a Finger to Change Positions

Pentatonic Scale Exercise with Position Changes

Open-String Tuning 1=D (5 1 2 5)

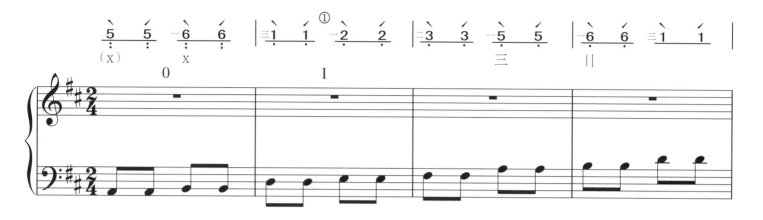

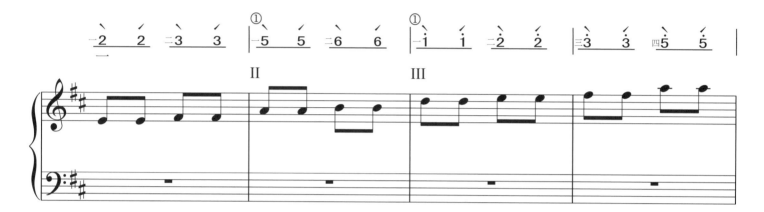

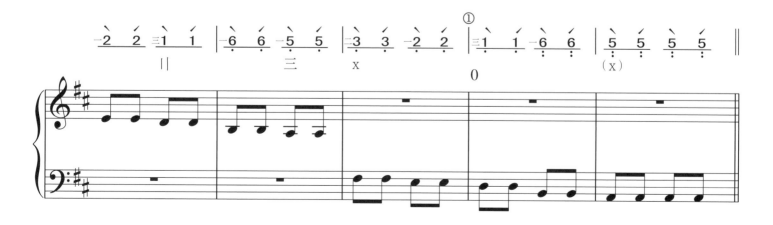

Two more kinds of position changes: **switching fingers on the same note to change positions**, and **jumping to positions not adjacent to each other** (e.g., from *Xiang* "O" position to position II).

The position changes are numbered in the following example:

③ Switching Fingers on the Same Note to Change Positions

④ Jumping to Positions Not Adjacent to Each Other

Open-String Tuning 1=D (5 1 2 5)

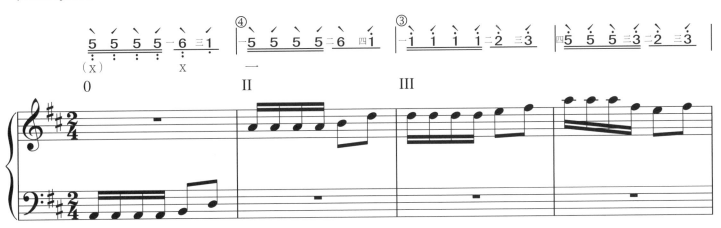

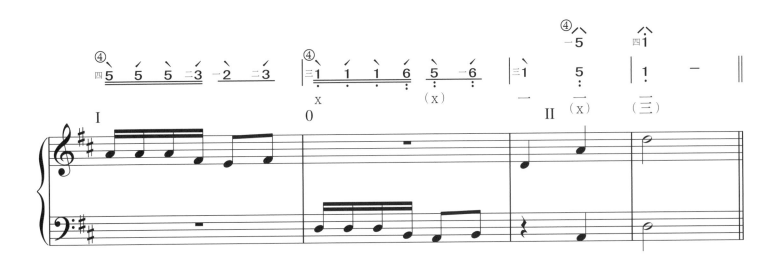

HISTORY OF THE CHINESE PIPA

The pipa is over 2000 years old in Chinese history. One of most widely used plucked stringed instruments in China, the pipa can be used in court music, classical music, folk music, and to accompany local operas. The early stages of pipa included a straight-neck pipa and a curved-neck pipa. Some older versions had five strings.

Five-String Pipa

Curved-Neck Pipa

TREMOLO / LUN ZHI

Lun Zhi (輪指) ⠿ is one of the most important techniques used in pipa playing. It's like the tremolo picking technique on classical guitar, though on the pipa it is played differently. Instead of plucking the fingers toward you with the fingertips, on the pipa, you pluck the strings with your nails pushing away from you. You pluck your fingers in a downward motion, while your thumb plucks the string with the nail in an upward motion. This technique starts with the index finger unless noted otherwise. There are several types of pipa *Lun Zhi*.

SAN ZHI LUN

San Zhi Lun (三指輪) ⠿ (three-finger tremolo) is like playing *Tan* and *Tiao*, then adding the middle finger *Ti* in between.
(**Ti** is when the right-hand middle finger plucks the string with a downward motion.)

San Zhi Lun Three-Finger Tremolo Exercise

VIDEOS 33–34
(left hand/right hand)

Open-String Tuning 1=D (5̣ 1̣ 2̣ 5)

SI ZHI LUN / BAN LUN

To achieve a **Si Zhi Lun** 四指輪 / 半輪 ❖ (four-finger tremolo or half tremolo) technique, pluck your fingers downward in succession. You start with your index finger and continue with your middle finger, ring finger, and finally pinky.

Your right hand should be held in a natural position, as if you were holding an egg. Avoid holding your hand so tight that the egg could break, or so loose that the egg could fall out of your hand.

After plucking the individual fingers, relax them in the air until you have used them all. Then return all four fingers to a natural loose-fist position as if you were holding an egg.

Correct

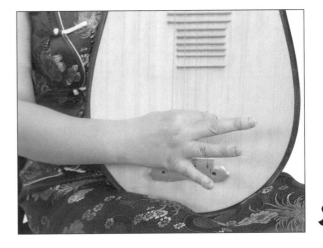

Incorrect

FOUR FAMOUS PIPA SCHOOLS

Pipa schools refer to different styles of playing pipa. These traditions were found in different regions of China and eventually developed into schools. The most famous pipa schools are:

1. **Pudong**, founded by Ju Shilin (also called Ju Pipa) from Shanghai Pudong Huinan town. In the 1950s, Lin Shicheng, the heir of *Pudong*, recomposed the pipa scores into Western notation and *Jianpu*. He wrote and edited textbooks containing *Pudong* pieces that were selected for the Central Conservatory of Music in Beijing. Widely recognized as the leading authority on *Pudong*, he passed away in 2005.

2. **Pinghu** is associated with the *Li Collection*, first published in 1895 and compiled by Li Fangyuan. It was the first pipa school to allow the use of the left-hand thumb and pinky.

3. **Chongming** is associated with *Old Melodies of Yingzhou*, compiled by Shen Zhaozhou in 1916.

4. The **Wang** or **Shanghai** school (named after the pipa master Wang Yuting) is considered a synthesis of the other three schools, especially the *Pudong* and *Pinghu* schools. It's the youngest pipa school. The *Wang* school is the only pipa school named after a pipa master rather than a region.

Si Zhi Lun Four-Finger Tremolo Exercise

After plucking with each finger, return them to a relaxed position in the air. Do not stiffen your fingers.

After finishing the first four-finger *Lun*, return your fingers to the original position and start the second four-finger *Lun* in the exact same way you started the first.

Open-String Tuning 1=D (5 1 2 5)

VIDEOS 35–36
(left hand/right hand)

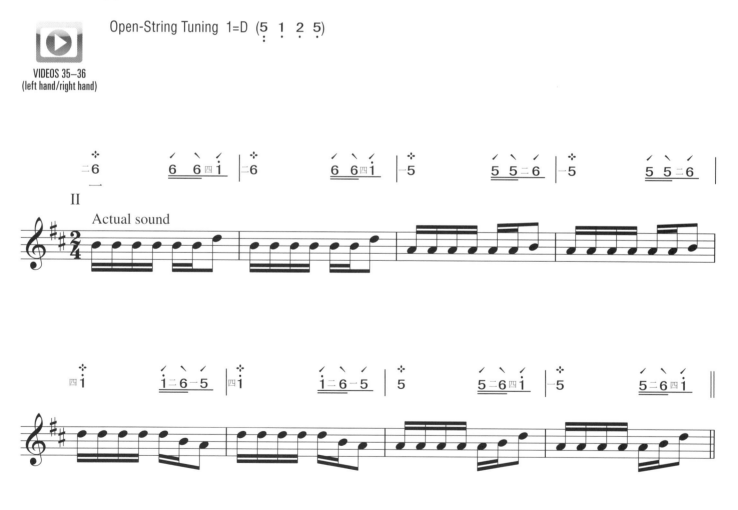

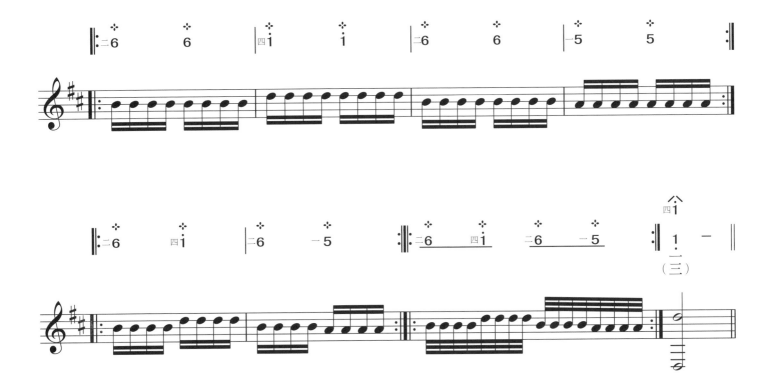

COMBINING TECHNIQUES

When playing on the same strings and with the same left- and right-hand fingering techniques, the notations will not be marked on the score for each individual note. Techniques used in the first measure will continue throughout subsequent measures until new techniques are indicated. But since this book is for beginners, an exception was made and many techniques are reiterated in the notation.

When playing right-hand techniques such as *Zhe, Fen, Shuang Tan,* or *Shuang Tiao,* the techniques already indicate that double notes are used. If a double note is on an open string, the note is not always written in the Chinese score, as shown here:

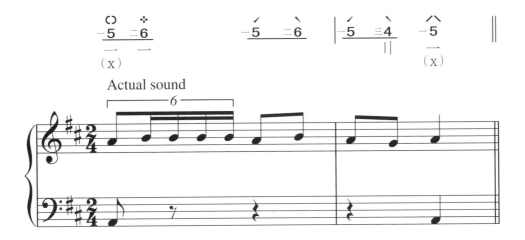

"Golden Snake Dance" combines *Tan, Tiao, Shuang Tan, Zhe, Fen, Sao,* and *Ban Lun* techniques. Start at a slow tempo. Keeping the tempo consistent is most important, regardless of whether you are playing eighth or sixteenth notes.

GOLDEN SNAKE DANCE
金蛇狂舞

Nie Er 聶耳
Arr. Gao Hong 高虹定琵琶指法

♩ = 116   Open-String Tuning 1=D (5 1 2 5)

VIDEOS 37–38
(left hand/right hand)

WU ZHI LUN / FIVE-FINGER TREMOLO

Wu Zhi Lun / Quan Lun ⁝ 五指輪/全輪 — Five-Finger Tremolo or Whole Tremolo

There are two kinds of five-finger tremolos:

1. **Shi Zhi Qi Ban Wu Zhi Lun** (食指起板五指輪), starting with the index finger:

*I M R P T
食 中無名小大 (指)

*I=Index Finger; M=Middle Finger; R=Ring Finger; P=Pinky; T=Thumb

2. **Da Zhi Qi Ban Wu Zhi Lun** (大指起板五指輪), starting with the thumb:

*T I M R P
大 食 中無名小 (指)

Five-finger tremolo is the most difficult technique on the pipa, and also the most important. The most commonly used five-finger tremolo starts with the index finger. Starting with the thumb is rare, but much easier for beginning students to start with. It's like playing a *Tiao* (挑) and adding a four-finger tremolo *Si Zhi Lun* (四指輪). Since you already learned the *Tiao* and *Si Zhi Lun* in past lessons, we will begin with five-finger tremolo exercises that start with the thumb: *Da Zhi Qi Ban Wu Zhi Lun* (大指起板五指).

Da Zhi Qi Ban Wu Zhi Lun Five-Finger Lun Starting with the Thumb

In the following exercise, start slowly and practice each finger independently. The volume produced by the thumb needs to be controlled and very soft. All five fingers must play at a consistent, steady speed, at the same volume level, and with the same articulation. The right wrist should be relaxed and the tips of the fingerpicks should be used to pluck the strings.

The first measure indicates the use of the left-hand index finger for both strings and notes on the same fret. Flatten your index finger to cover both strings at the same time. This is the only time you don't need to press the string with your fingertip!

VIDEOS 39–41
(left hand/right hand/fast)

Open-String Tuning 1=D (5 1 2 5)

Shi Zhi Qi Ban Wu Zhi Lun Five-Finger Lun Starting with the Index Finger

Because your fingers are different lengths and vary in strength, control must be used to produce a unified sound. The index finger and thumb naturally play louder in comparison to the softer ring finger and pinky. Therefore, you should begin practicing at a very slow tempo, trying to control the volume on each finger. The result should be a smooth and steady sound at a consistent volume level. Here is an example of how to practice the five-finger tremolo at a slow tempo while counting the numbers 1, 2, 3, 4, 5.

VIDEO 42

The following exercise has two important elements that will help you in practicing left-hand and right-hand coordination. Starting at a slow tempo, play one note at a time with both hands. After you can play each note well at a slow pace, speed up the tempo. Even if you can play them very well, I would still highly recommend continuing to practice this exercise every day from this point on. This practice will provide long-term benefits in the execution of your *Lun* technique.

VIDEOS 43–44
(left hand/right hand)

Open-String Tuning 1=D (5 1 2 5)

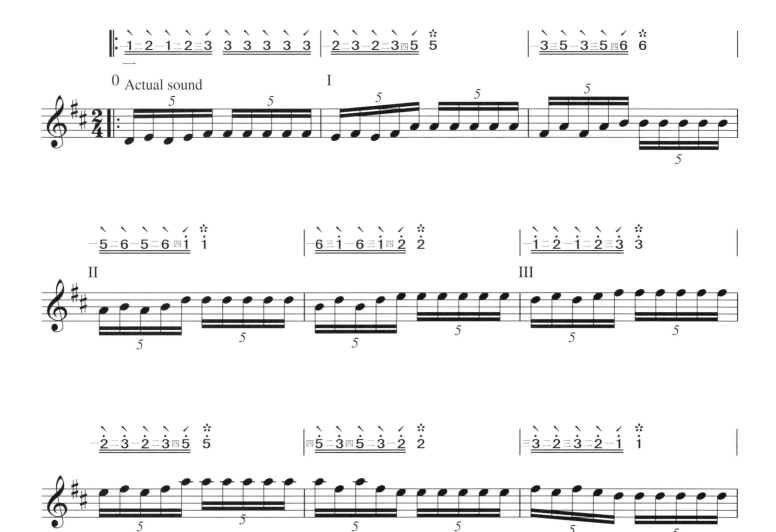

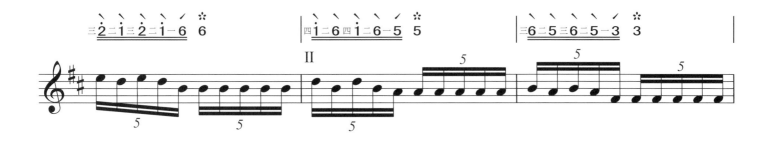

CHANG LUN FIVE-FINGER LONG TREMOLO AND GUN ZHI

Chang Lun 長輪 � . . . . .

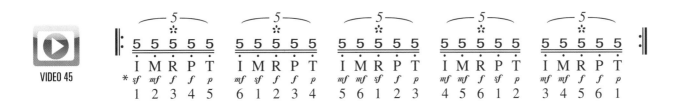

Chang in Chinese means "long time." **Chang Lun** means combining many five-finger tremolos in a row without stopping, resulting in one long tremolo. This is the most difficult technique on the pipa, and it is mostly used on the first string. It will take at least three to six months to smoothly connect the *Lun* to a long tremolo. Please do not get discouraged by the slow process. To make it easier to go between first and second *Lun*, you can count in 6 instead of 5. On each 1, play the 1 louder than the other numbers. Here is an example of how to practice on the first open string at a slow tempo while counting the numbers 1, 2, 3, 4, 5, 6.

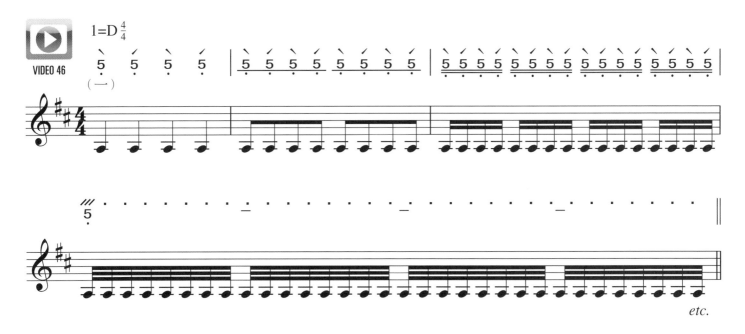

* Index and middle fingers play in medium loud volume *mf*; ring finger and pinky play in loud volume *f*; thumb plays only in soft volume *p*. On "1," play extra loud *sf*; except when the "1" is played on the thumb.

Gun Zhi 滾指 /// . . . . .

Gun Zhi is *Tan* and *Tiao* at fast tempo, and a combination of several *Gun Zhi* in a row without stopping, resulting in one long tremolo. This kind of tremolo is mostly used on the second, third, and fourth strings. Here is an example of how to practice going from *Tan* and *Tiao* into the fast-paced *Gun Zhi*:

As you begin your practice of *Chang Lun*, play at a slow tempo to make sure the sounds produced by each finger are balanced both in volume and in execution. The sound should be smooth and the notes should be steady.

Try to keep whole *Lun* (five-finger tremolo) on each quarter note (one beat). If there are four beats, you play four whole *Lun*. If there are two beats, play two whole *Lun*, etc. After your fingers start producing a smooth and steady sound, you can gradually speed up and double the whole *Lun* tremolos: two whole *Luns* for one beat, eight whole *Luns* for four beats, and so on.

Chang Lun is the most difficult technique on the pipa, so don't worry if your five fingers don't produce a smooth and balanced sound right away. Keep practicing every day, and you will get better!

"Colored Clouds Chasing the Moon" combines *Chang Lun* and *Gun Zhi* techniques.

COLORED CLOUDS CHASING THE MOON (EXCERPT) 彩雲追月片段

Very important note for tremolo techniques:

These lessons provide instruction for the most important pipa tremolo techniques. These techniques typically take at least two years to master, so don't be discouraged if your progress is slow. It is important to learn these techniques early on, and that is why the tremolo basics are included in this book at this point. Only a few tremolo exercises are included to prevent you from getting discouraged or stalled. The exercises included in this book were written to provide the most effective way to learn these techniques. They were developed after a lifelong regimen of daily practice. Learning these techniques is an ongoing process, and practicing them every day for at least 20 minutes from now on is highly recommended. This will prepare you for playing the intermediate-level pieces at the end of the book.

NOTE BENDING

There are a wide variety of note-bending techniques on the pipa. The **Tui** and **La/Wan** techniques are similar to note bending in guitar music.

TUI

Tui (推) ("push") ↗ is achieved when one of your left-hand fingers presses a string on a fret, the note is plucked, and the finger is pushed to your right side. There are two kinds of *Tui*:

Shang Tui ↗ (上推)

Shang Tui is achieved by plucking a note on a string, pushing the string towards you to reach a higher pitch, then releasing it back to the original pitch. This is most often used on the first or second strings and in the first position (I).

In the following example, pay attention to the differences between the first- and second-line *Tui* techniques. The first line is a fast *Tui*, and you must release the bend quickly to play the next note with the right hand. This is called **Shi Tui Yin** or **Shi Hua Yin** (實推音或實滑音).

In the second line *Tui*, you pluck only the first note, then push to the next note without the use of the right hand (i.e., without plucking). This is called **Xu Tui Yin** or **Xu Hua Yin** (虛推音或虛滑音).

Xia Tui ↘ (下推)

In this technique, before plucking, you bend the string towards you to a higher pitch and *then* pluck the string with a right-hand finger. Release the note after plucking it, allowing it to fall back onto the fret and back to the original pitch. This is like a pre-bend in guitar music. It is most often used on the first string and in the first position (I).

Pay close attention to the notes that start each *Xia Tui*. In general, the rules for such techniques are to begin with the next higher note found in the Chinese five-tone pentatonic scale. The actual sounds are shown in the Western notation.

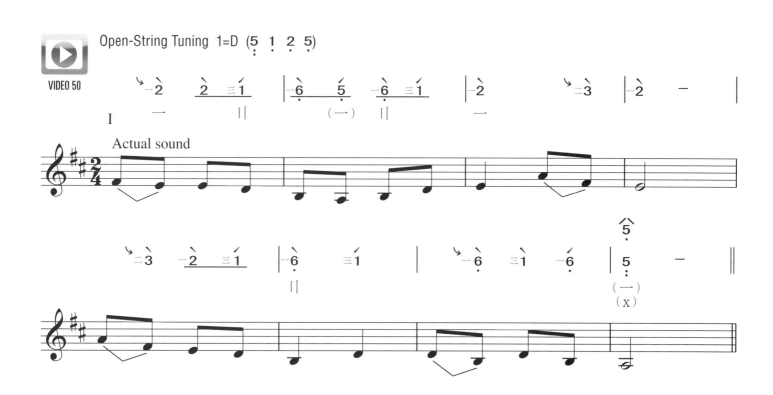

Open-String Tuning 1=D (5 1 2 5)

LA/WAN

In **La/Wan** ↗ (拉/挽) ("pull") technique, one of your left-hand fingers presses a string near a fret and then you pull the finger away from you to your left side, raising the pitch. There are two kinds of *La/Wan*:

Shang La/Wan ↗ (上拉 / 挽)

Pull the string from a lower pitch to a higher pitch, then release it back to the original pitch. This can be used on all four strings and in the second (II) and third (III) positions. In Chinese notation, *Shang La/Wan* is placed *after* the note.

Xia La/Wan ↘ (下拉 / 挽)

This technique is achieved by: 1) pulling the string away from you to a higher pitch; 2) plucking the string; then 3) releasing the string, allowing it to fall back to the original pitch. This can be used on all four strings and in the second (II) and third (III) positions. In Chinese notation, *Xia La/Wan* is placed *before* the note.

"Flying Kites" includes *Shang La/Wan* and *Xia La/Wan* techniques. Note that:

① is *Xu Hua Yin* (虛滑音); do not pluck the 5 (sol) with the right hand. Just bend up to it.

② is *Shi Hua Yin* (實滑音); pluck the right-hand note first, then bend to the pitch on the score.

FLYING KITES 放風箏

Jiangnan Folk Tune 江南民歌

Arr. Gao Hong 高虹定指法

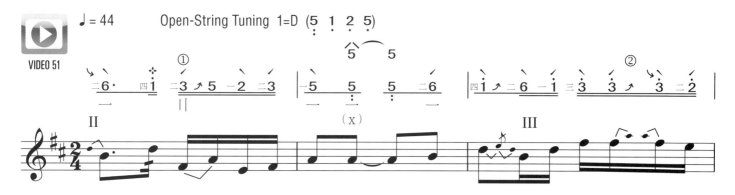

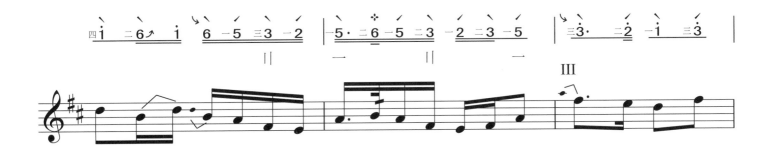

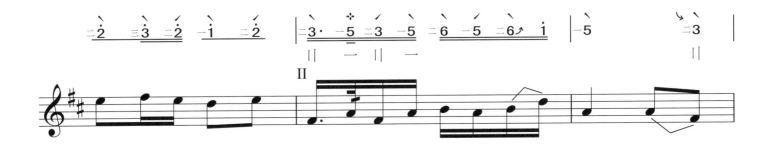

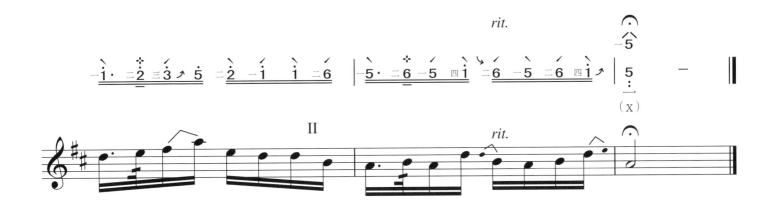

VIBRATO AND OVERTONES

There are two kinds of vibrato, **Yin** (吟) and **Rou** (揉).

YIN

VIDEO 52

For **Yin** (吟) ◆ ("old-fashioned vibrato"), the left-hand finger presses the string near a fret and swings evenly from left to right. There are four kinds of *Yin* vibrato:

①   **Small Vibrato**   ◆   (小吟) :   Swing with a small movement.

②   **Large Vibrato**   ◆   (大吟) :   Swing with a large movement.

③   **Fast Vibrato**   ◆   (快吟) :   Swing with a fast movement.

④   **Slow Vibrato**   ◆   (慢吟) :   Swing with a slow movement.

All *Yin* are marked with the same symbol. For common usage, the small and fast vibratos are for eighth notes, and the large and slow vibratos are for half notes or whole notes. Also, usage is based on the needs of the music. Sometimes, the *Yin* starts with a small and fast vibrato and then changes to a large and slow vibrato, or vise versa. These changes in usage are not written down on the scores. We will discuss more details as we learn new pieces and examine the needs of each piece.

ROU

Rou (揉) ("new-fashioned vibrato"): a left-hand finger presses the string near a fret and swings with a movement going from left to right and then up and down. Playing this technique feels like pressing a string and doing a circular movement on the string.

Notes:

When you play the *Yin*, the swing from left to right must be done evenly. It's very common to pull more than push. Make sure the finger returns back to the original pitch; otherwise, the intonation will be too high.

If the *Yin* or *Rou* vibrato is in the *Xiang* position (0), do not swing left to right or up and down due to the shorter frets. Instead, you will need to press the string downward to the fret to make the sound a little higher, then release the finger to allow the sound to go back to the original pitch.

In "Jasmine Flower," *Yin* markings appear in the notation. *Rou* (揉) can be used anytime, so there are no markings for it. After mastering the *Yin*, we will work on the new-fashioned vibrato *Rou*.

JASMINE FLOWER 茉莉花

♩ = 70   Open-String Tuning 1=D (5 1 2 5)

Hebei Folk Tune 河北民歌
Arr. Gao Hong 高虹定指法

VIDEO 53

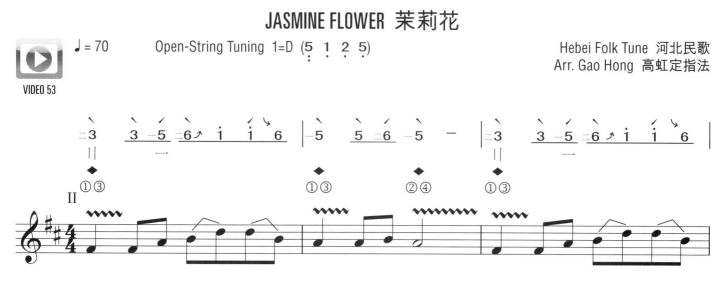

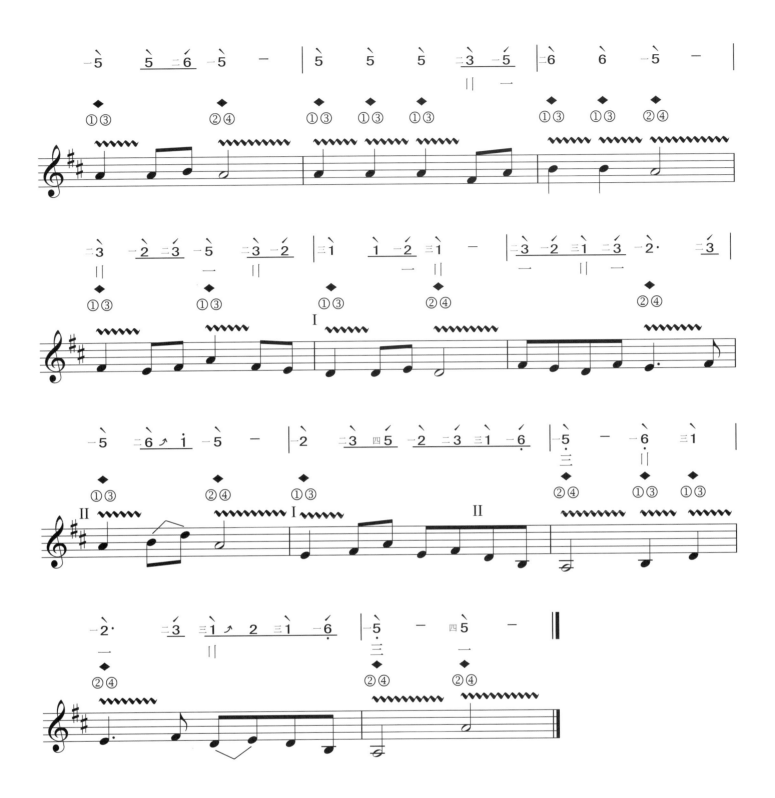

FANYIN (OVERTONES)

An **overtone** (or harmonic) is produced by plucking a string with the right hand while the left-hand finger barely touches the string directly above the fret for the desired note. It's the same concept as producing harmonics on Western stringed instruments, and the harmonic system is identical; it only happens at particular places along the string (shown here).

To produce the best overtone sound, press lightly with the left hand and pluck hard with the right hand. After plucking with the right hand first, quickly lift your left hand off the string to make the sound ring clearly. Avoid lifting your left hand off the string at the exact same time as plucking with your right hand; there should be a slight delay.

Natural Overtones for the Key of D

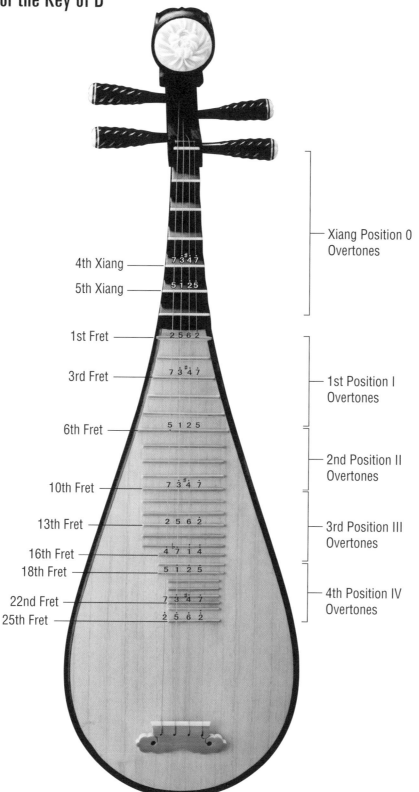

Here are the **Fanyin** (泛音 °) overtone positions for the following piece, "Three Variations of Plum Blossoms":

1̊ – 6th fret on the third string

2̊ – 6th fret on the second string

5̊ – 1st fret on the third string

6̊ – 1st fret on the second string

1̊ – Octave higher – 5th *Xiang* (0 position) on the third string

3̊ – 3rd fret on the third string

5̊ – Octave lower – 6th fret on the fourth string

To make the overtone clearer and brighter, the left-hand fingers need to touch the string lightly while the right hand plucks the string strongly. A common mistake is to play both hands with the same force.

THREE VARIATIONS OF PLUM BLOSSOMS 梅花三弄

♩ = 58   Open-String Tuning 1=D (5̣ 1̣ 2̣ 5̣)

Ancient 古曲

Arr. Gao Hong 高虹定指法

VIDEO 54

The remaining portions of this book will introduce the keys of C and G and pipa sound effects.

Option: If you feel confident that you have mastered all the techniques up to this point, you can jump ahead to "Purple Bamboo" and "Thunder in a Dry Season."

THE KEY OF C

Key of C Positions

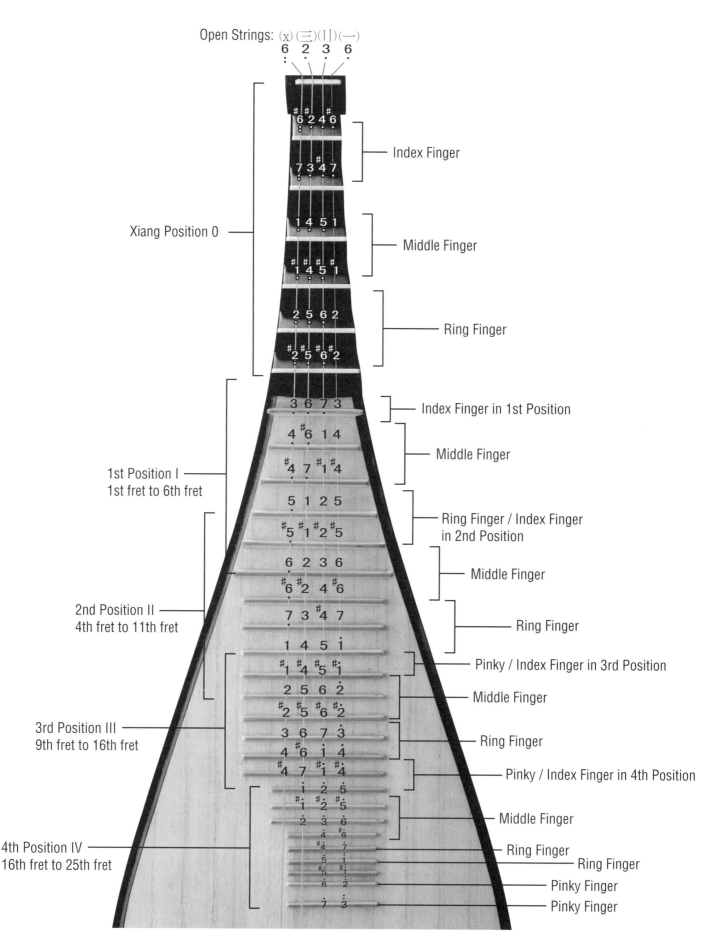

Open Strings: (x)(三)(‖)(一)

In the following exercise, every time you change positions, there are four sixteenth notes that appear. Use this transition to remind you to prepare for the position changes and to help you remember the positions.

This exercise marks the first time you will use the fourth position (IV). When playing in the fourth position, the left-hand thumb can be brought up on the front of the pipa, as shown:

DRUM SONG FROM FENGYANG 鳳陽花鼓

An Hui Folk Tune 安徽民歌
Arr. Gao Hong 高虹定指法

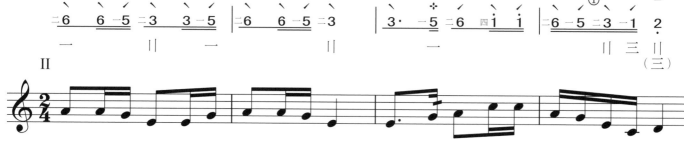

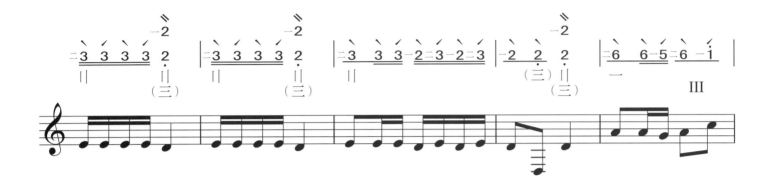

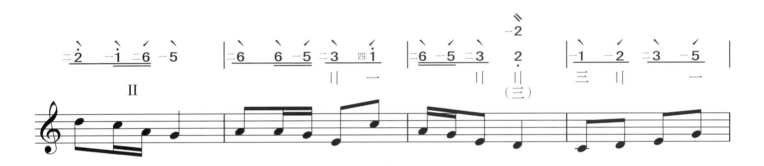

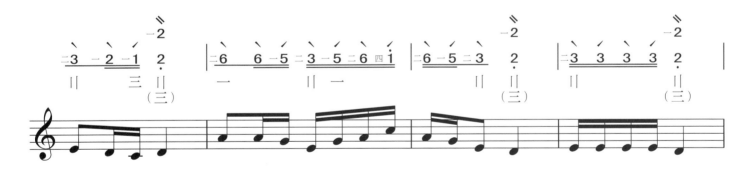

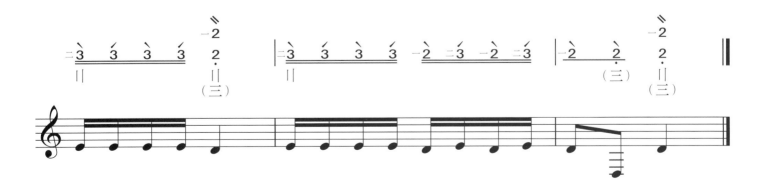

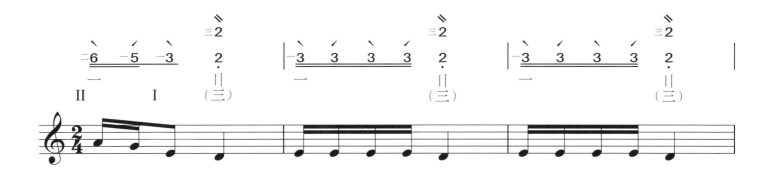

*① can also be played in the first position (I) like this:

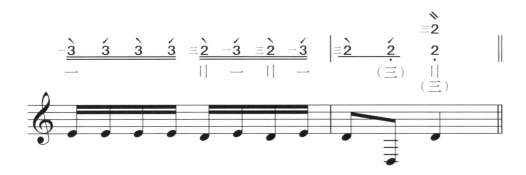

THE KEY OF G

Key of G Positions

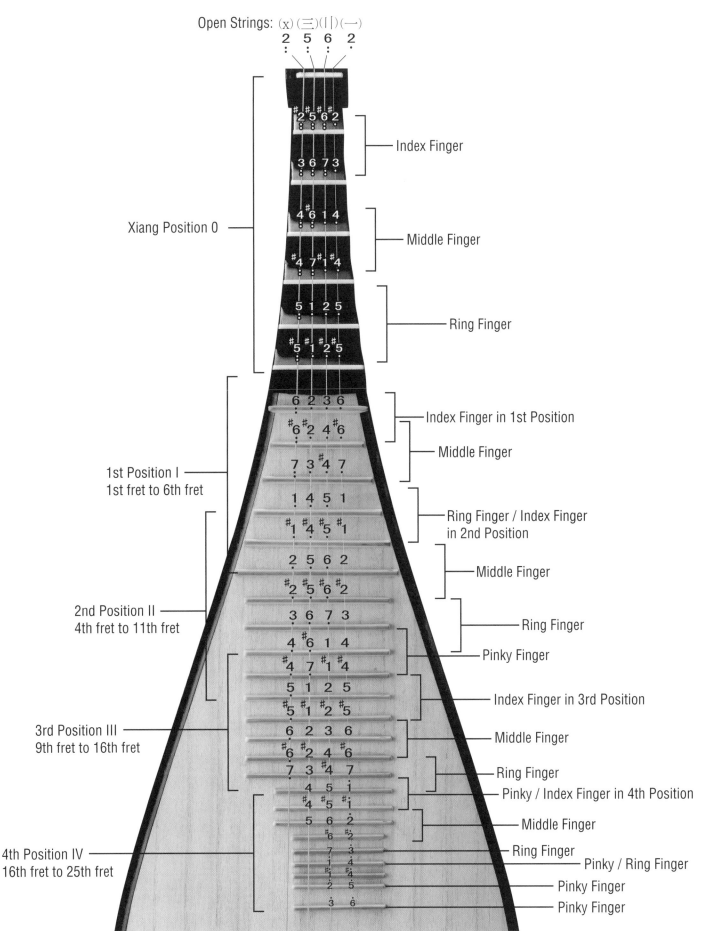

In this key of G exercise, every time you change positions, there is a quarter note that appears. Use this to prepare for the position changes and to help you remember the positions.

Key of G All Positions Exercise

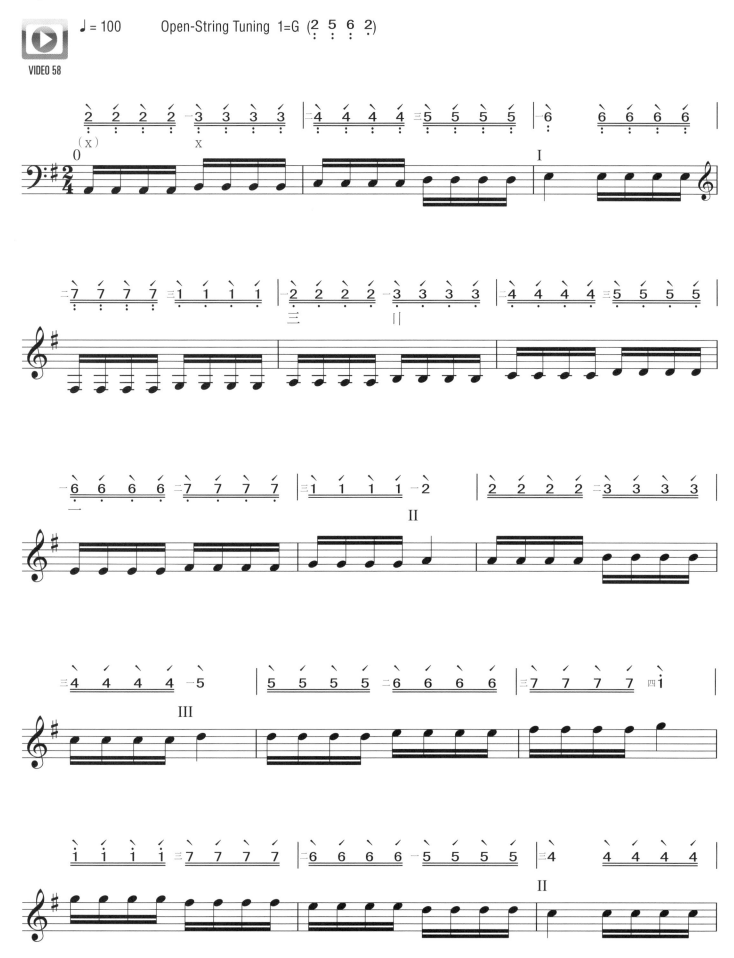

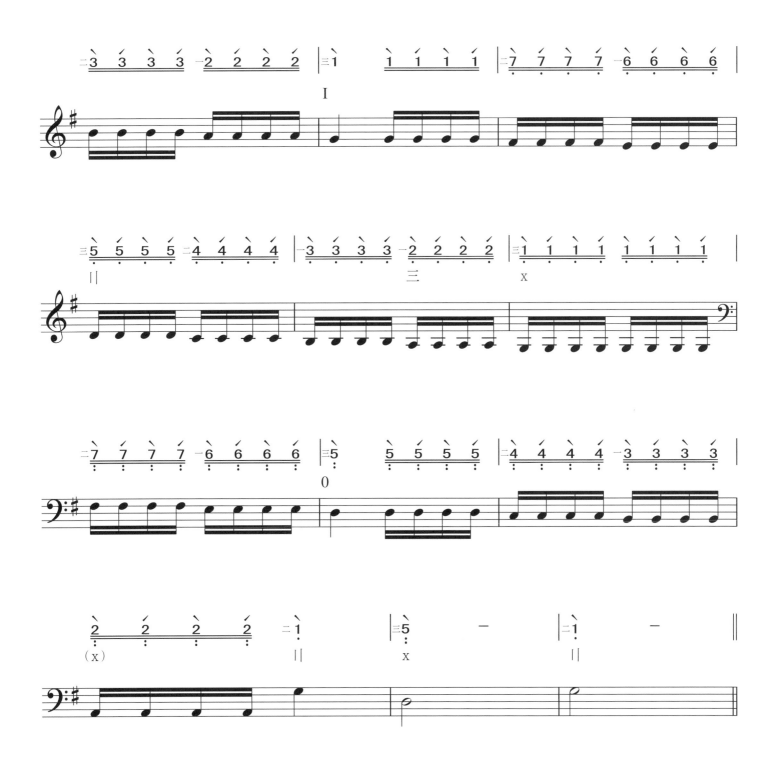

In the next tune, "Selling Rice Balls," there are a few options for playing certain notes and phrases, as indicated with numbers:

① This "6" (la) can also be played by the pinky while staying in the second position (II). If the pinky is used in this measure, the entire measure can be played in the second position (II).

When there are different options for playing a passage, the choice of which to use should be based on the ease of play and the option that best keeps a consistent tone quality throughout the passage. You can try both options to see which best fits for your hand and the music. This arrangement of "Selling Rice Balls" is an exercise piece, so you should try it both ways and make your choice. When you become an advanced player, you will need to decide your own positions and fingering yourself, since most scores in advanced repertoire do not contain markings for fingerings and positions.

SELLING RICE BALLS 賣湯圓

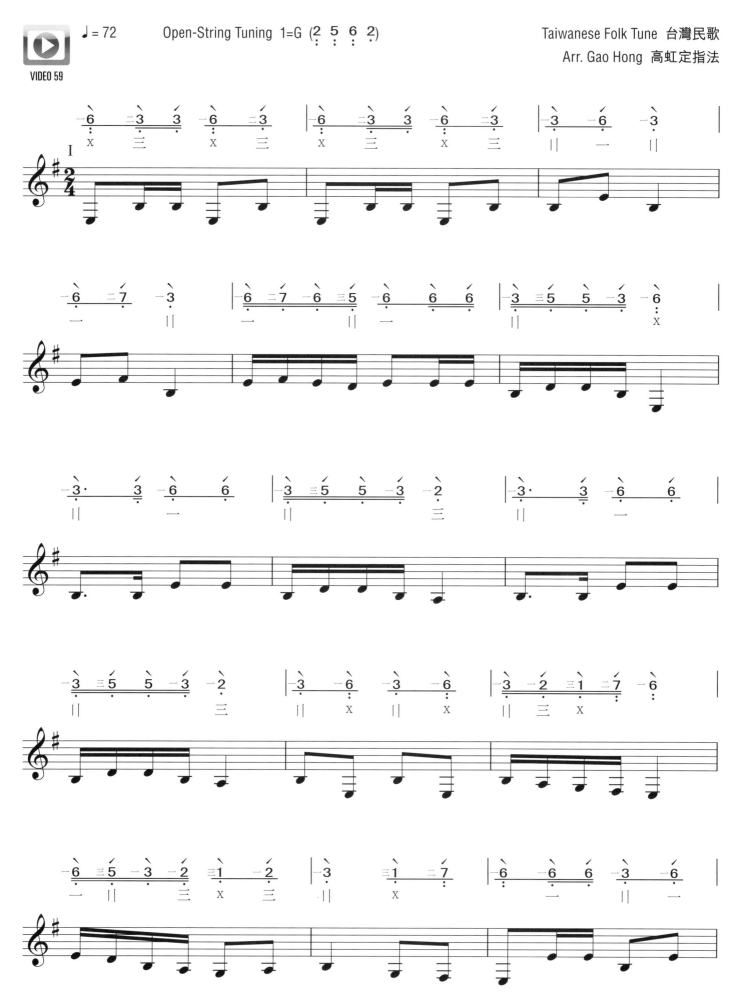

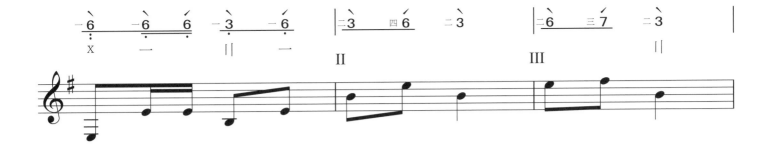

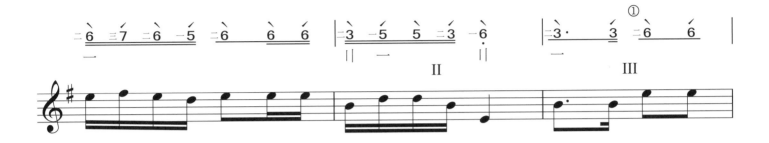

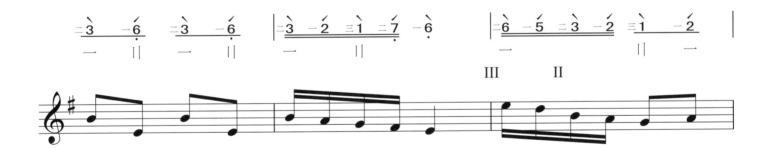

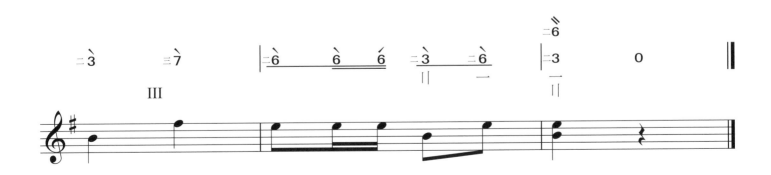

RIGHT-HAND SOUND EFFECT TECHNIQUES

ARPEGGIOS / GUA AND LIN

The first of many sound effect techniques you will learn on the pipa, **arpeggios** are chords played one note at a time, with upward or downward movement.

In **Pa Yin** (琶音) ⟨ techniques, the right-hand index finger or thumb plucks the strings downward or upward to produce effects imitating the sound of flowing water. There are two essential ways to play this kind of arpeggio:

1. **Gua** (挂) ⟨ —also known as **Hua** (划): The right-hand index finger plucks from the fourth string to the first string with a downward motion.

2. **Lin** (臨) ⟨ : The right-hand thumb plucks from the first string to the fourth string with an upward motion.

When playing a harmony that calls for two or three notes to be played simultaneously, as in "Flying Song," you will need to flatten the finger(s) to assure all the notes are being properly pressed.

FLYING SONG 飛歌

Open-String Tuning 1=C (6̣ 2̣ 3̣ 6̣)

Miao (Hmong) Folk Tune 苗族民歌

Arr. Gao Hong 高虹改編

VIDEOS 60–61
(left hand/right hand)

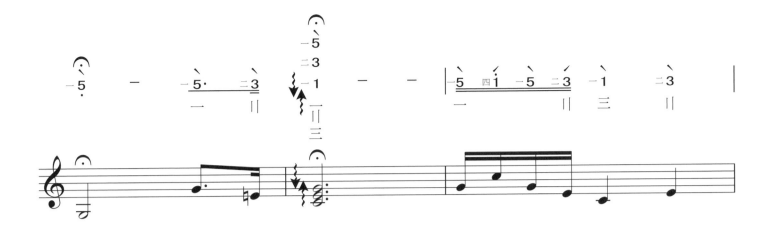

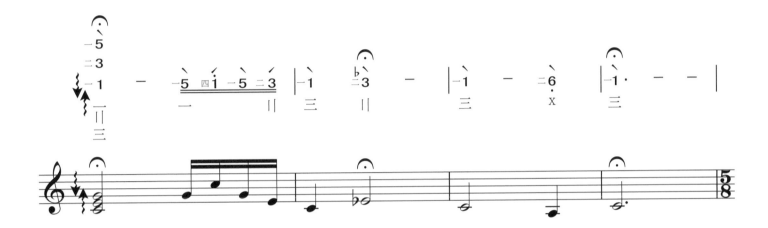

Fast

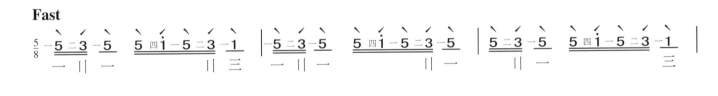

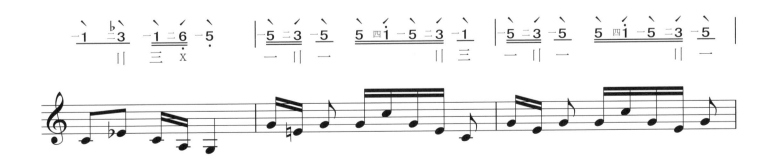

GEOGRAPHY, DIALECTS, AND LIFESTYLES IN CHINESE MUSIC

Chinese melodies are strongly influenced by dialects; dialects in turn are influenced by geography, and peoples' personalities, cultures, and lifestyles.

Northern Music Style: In northern China, you find many mountains and open fields. When people talk, their voices are loud and bright due to the hardships of their lives and their open personalities. Loud voices and shouting are also necessary for communicating in the mountains and open fields. That's why most northern-style instruments are high-pitched, such as the *Banhu* (a bowed string instrument with a coconut resonator), *Jinghu* (a bowed fiddle used in Peking Opera), *Suona* (an oboe-like wind instrument), and others. Like the tonal inflections of northern dialects, the melodies contain large skips from note to note. If you were to draw the melodies, you would clearly see the shapes of mountains. Northern music is always exciting and dramatic, describing the happiness and hardships of the lives of the people.

Melodic lines in northern music resemble the shapes of mountains:

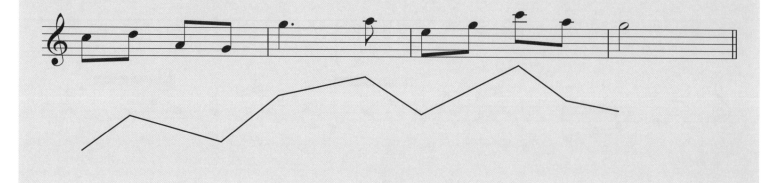

Southern Music Style: In southern China there are many beautiful rivers and dense populations. People need to lower their voices, and their dialects have more syllables and tones making their speech smoother. Like these dialects, southern-style instruments are much quieter. The melodic twists and turns occur within a small range and resemble casual conversation. Here you won't find the large melodic skips of northern melodies. If you were to draw southern melodies graphically, the lines would resemble the meandering of rivers. Due to the beautiful landscapes, unique cultures, and exquisite lifestyles of the southern people, this music resembles Chinese landscape paintings and is full of pleasant, flowing elegance and beauty.

Melodic lines in southern music resemble the shapes of rivers:

ZHAI, PAI, TI, AND TAN MIANBAN TECHNIQUES

VIDEO 62

1. **Zhai** (摘) ✗ : The right-hand thumbnail presses on the string, and the index or middle finger plucks the string at the same time to produce a bright, percussive sound, such as the sound of a horse trotting or the ticking of a clock.

2. **Pai** (拍) **L** : The right-hand thumb pulls up on the fourth string quickly and loudly to produce a loud slapping sound, such as the sound of an explosion or cannon shot.

3. **Ti** (提) **K** : The right-hand thumb and index finger hold one string together, lifts it up, and slaps it back quickly and loudly to produce a surprising explosive sound, such as a gunshot or cannon shot. Though similar to *Pai*, *Ti* can be accomplished on any string, while *Pai* can only be done on the fourth string.

4. **Tan Mianban** (彈面板) **⊢** : The right-hand index and/or middle fingernails are used to strike the wood on the lower part of the pipa belly to produce a bright popping sound like the sound of fireworks.

"Yi Folk Tune" is an exercise in *Zhai, Pai, Ti,* and *Tan Mianban* techniques. When playing passages that contain both plucked notes and sound effects, make sure that during the transitions the rhythm remains consistent and the pulse steady.

When playing *Tan Mianban* (彈面板) **⊢** make sure to strike the belly of the pipa with your full nail hitting the wood, and not just the tip of your nail. This will assure that the sound is loud and bright. The striking position should not be too close to the edge of the pipa. Find the place on the belly that makes the loudest sound.

YI FOLK TUNE 彝族民歌

♩ = 69 Open-String Tuning 1=D (5 1 2 5) Arr. Gao Hong 高虹改編

LEFT-HAND SPECIAL TECHNIQUES

DA, SOU, AND DAI

- **Da** (打) ▲ : Only a left-hand finger is used to hit the string on the note to produce a soft sound. No right-hand technique is used.

- **Sou** (擻) ❜ : Only a left-hand finger is used to pluck the string on the note to produce a soft sound. Again, no right-hand technique is used. Normally, one finger is pressing the note, and the next finger plucks the string. (For example, the index finger presses near the fret, middle finger plucks the string; or middle finger presses near the fret, ring finger plucks the string.)

- **Dai** (帶) ◡ : After right-hand finger plucks the string and the left-hand finger presses the string, the left-hand finger is lifted off the note quickly to produce a soft sound (without using the right hand to pluck the second note).

The difference between *Sou* and *Dai* is: *Sou* doesn't use the right hand to pluck the string, while *Dai* uses the right hand to pluck the first note, but the right hand is not used to produce the second. Be aware that it's very easy to confuse these two techniques.

Da, *Sou*, and *Dai* are commonly used in *Wen*-style music due to the soft volume of sound. The sounds produced are also called *Xu Yin* (虛音), meaning "delicate notes." In the following example, サ is an abbreviation of the Chinese character 散, which means to play freely (*rubato*).

① indicates *Dai* (帶) ◡ in the following score. There are two fingering marks on the same notation: one for the plucked first note, and the other for the note sounded when the left-hand index finger is kept near the fret, and the middle finger is lifted quickly.

② indicates *Sou* (擻) ❜ and means that the left-hand index finger presses near the fret, then the left-hand middle finger is used to pluck the note without the right hand. Again, that's why there are two fingering marks on the same notation. (All the fingerings for *Dai* and *Sou* remain the same throughout the piece, though not all the fingerings are marked in the score.)

③ overtones are played on the *Xiang* position's fifth fret on the third string.

④ overtone is played on the *Xiang* position's fourth fret on the third string.

⑤ overtones are played on the first position's second fret on the third string.

CHANTING 起咒

Open-String Tuning 1=D (5̣ 1 2̇ 5̇)

Buddhist Temple Music 佛教音樂

VIDEOS 64–66
(left hand/right hand/both)

Free time

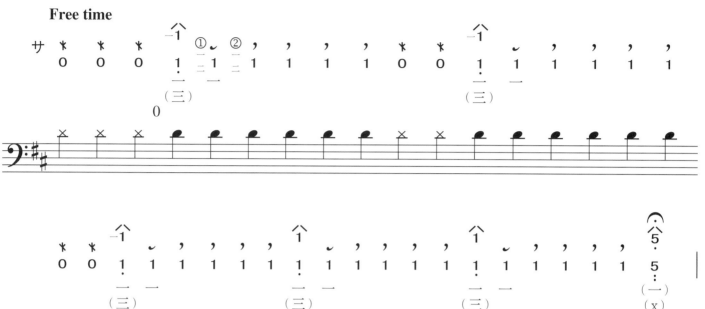

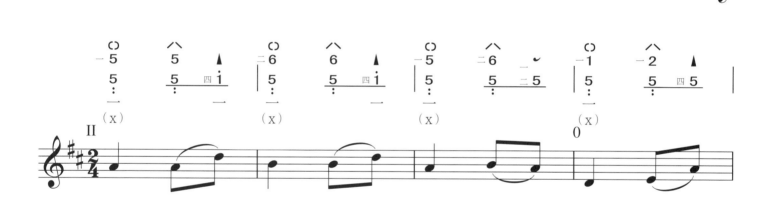

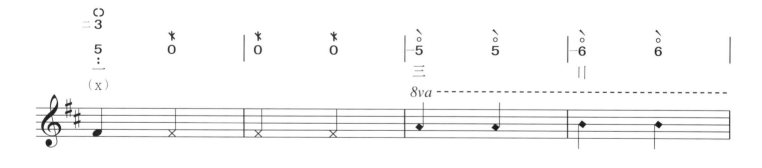

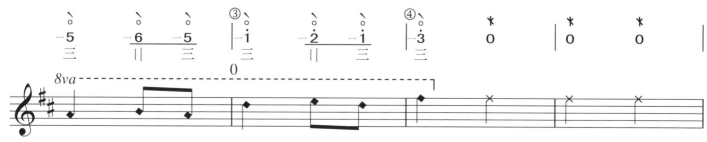

70

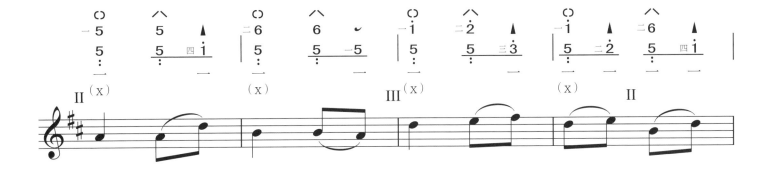

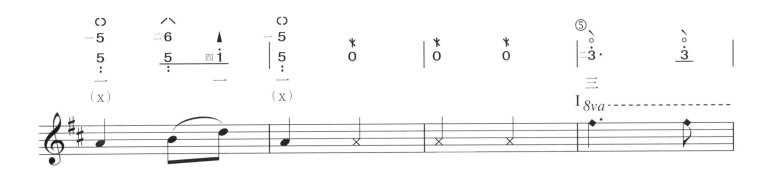

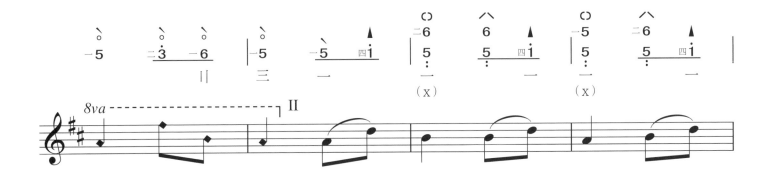

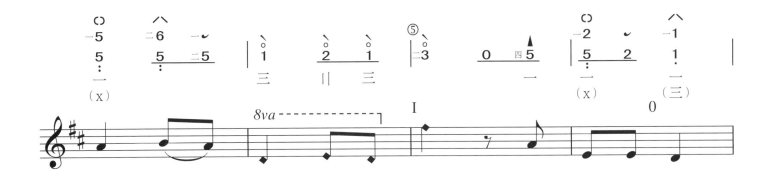

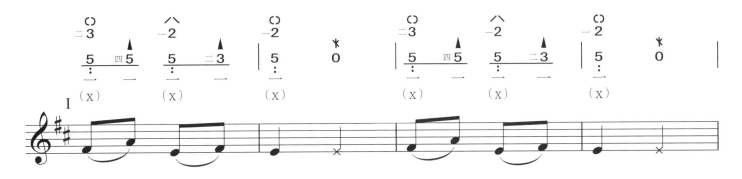

⑥ can also be played like this, as in the left- and right-hand videos:

right-hand video

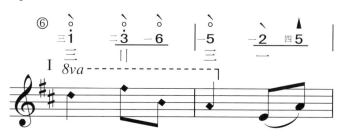

left-hand video

MORE SPECIAL TECHNIQUES

JIAO, SHA, AND FU

VIDEO 67

Jiao (絞) ⊬ : There are three kinds of *Jiao*. Since this book is for beginners, we will just learn one: the first string and second string *Jiao*. The left-hand ring finger pushes the first string under the second string, then pulls the second string to cross over the top of the first. The index finger then presses on both strings together to produce sound effects imitating Chinese gongs and other percussion instruments, horses neighing, people screaming, and other sounds of battle.

VIDEO 68

Sha (煞) ⊥ : A left-hand fingernail is placed under the string and presses against the string to produce a percussive effect that imitates swords clashing or other metal objects clanging together.

Fu (伏) ⊬⊬ : The left-hand or right-hand fingers cover the string, stopping the sound suddenly.

In "Celebration," ① indicates *Zhai* (摘) ⊬ which uses a four-finger *Lun* rather than a single finger to pluck the notes (see Video 62). The **D.S.** near the end of the piece tells you to return to the sign (𝄋) and play through again to the end.

CELEBRATION 慶豐收

♩ = 66   Open-String Tuning 1=C (6 2 3 6)

Gao Hong 高虹作曲

VIDEOS 69–71
(left hand/right hand/both)

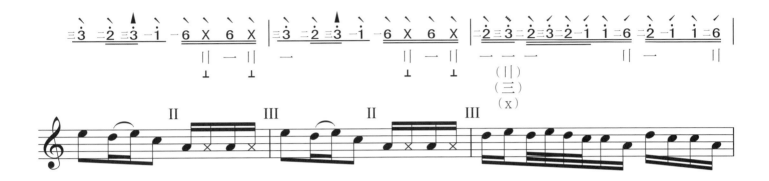

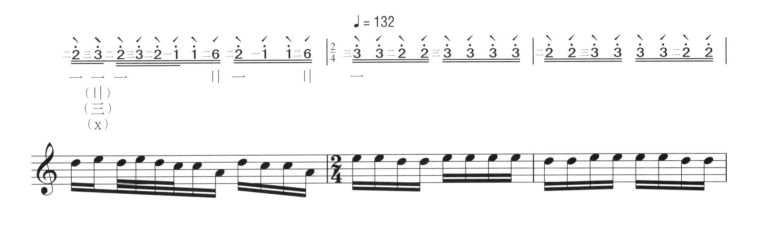

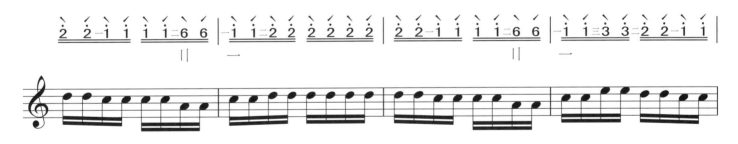

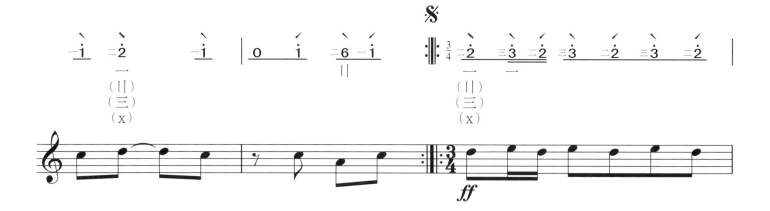

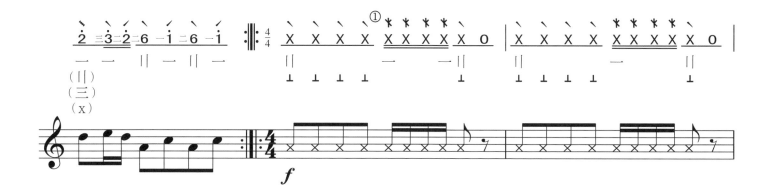

D.S.
(take repeats)

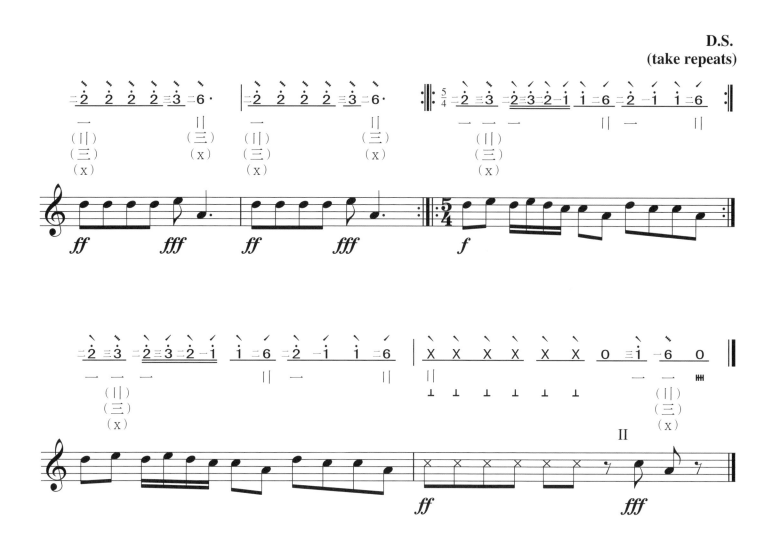

CHINESE SILK AND BAMBOO MUSIC

Silk and Bamboo refers to music played by string and wind instruments. Silk was the traditional material used for all strings in ancient China such as those for the erhu, pipa, etc. Bamboo was the material used to construct wind instruments such as the dizi, xiao, and sheng. There are two types of Silk and Bamboo music in China: **Jiangnan Sizhu** and **Guangdong Yinyue**.

JIANGNAN SIZHU

Jiangnan is the traditional name for the area spanning the southern portion of Jiangsu province, including the city of Shanghai, and northern Zhejiang province. *Jiangnan Sizhu* (江南絲竹) is considered to be a folk tradition. It's typically performed at informal gatherings, often at teahouses. The melodic line is beautiful, lively, happy, and smooth. The music reflects the beauty of the Jiangnan landscape and happiness of Jiangnan people.

Jiahua 加花

Jia means "to add," and *Hua* literally means "flowers." Silk and Bamboo music is full of ornamentations that make the music more exciting and lively. In fast passages, extra pentatonic (five-note scale) notes are added to the basic melody in both upward and downward directions, including grace notes and notes added to the melodic line. In slower passages, special techniques such as tremolos, trills, and note bends are used to alter and intensify the melody. The choice of ornamentation depends on what is natural to the instrument being played. For example, trills and grace notes are easy to produce on the dizi, erhu, and other string and wind instruments, while tremolos work well on plucked instruments, and note bends are most suitable for the pipa.

"Purple Bamboo" is one of the standard pieces in standard Pipa Level I exam requirement repertories in China. The playing of the same piece differs each time it is performed, depending on the influences and playing styles of the individual musicians involved. Here are some examples. After you have learned the piece, you can try adding some ornamentation of your own.

Basic Melody

1=D

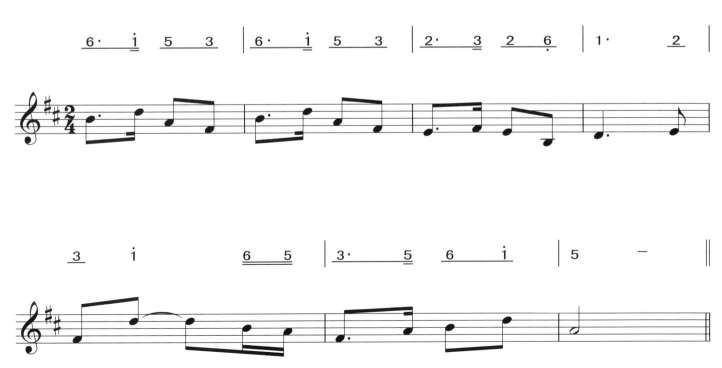

Jiahua sample for adding more notes:

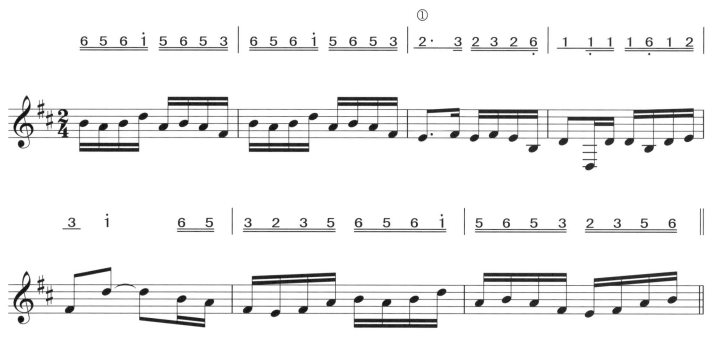

① can also add more notes such as:

Jiahua sample for adding ornamentation:

Some basic-level ornamentation is used in the following score of "Purple Bamboo."

"Purple Bamboo" combines most of the techniques you have learned so far. Take your time; start out at a slow tempo and gradually increase your speed as you become more comfortable with the notes and techniques.

When the long tremolo (*Chang Lun*) technique appears, do the following:

- If the note is a quarter note, play the five-finger *Lun* (*Quan Lun*) twice through starting with the index finger and ending with the thumb (as in measure 5).

- If the note is a half note, play the five-finger *Lun* four times through starting with the index finger and ending with the pinky (as in the last measure).

- If the note is a dotted eighth note, play the five-finger *Lun* one and a half times through, starting with the index finger and ending with the pinky, and connect it to the next *Tiao* (as in measure 7).

- After you master the piece at full speed using these techniques, you can begin to use tremolos more freely. No more counting is needed as long as the tremolos remain smooth and consistent and continue for the duration of each note. These guidelines should only be used as a beginning-level introduction to playing tremolos.

PURPLE BAMBOO 紫竹調

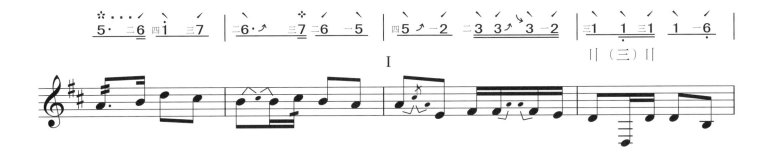

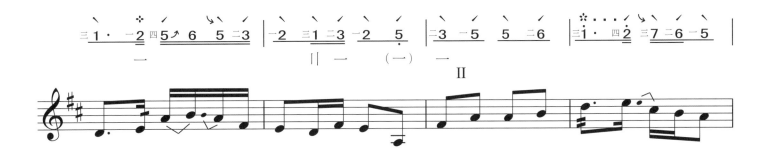

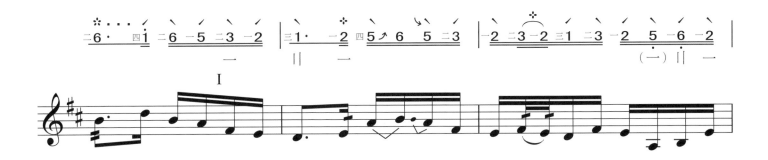

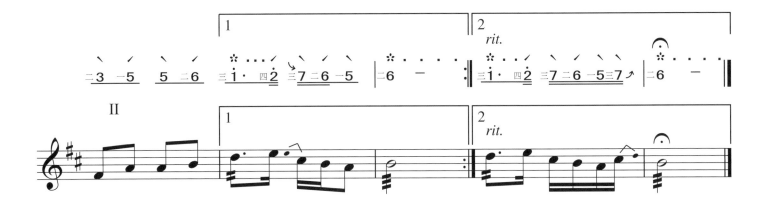

Video 72 shows "Purple Bamboo" played with a variety of special ornamentations based on Gao Hong's interpretation. In Video 73, you'll find the fully ornamented version.

GUANGDONG YINYUE

Guangdong Yinyue (廣東音樂) is a traditional style of Silk and Bamboo music, named for areas surrounding the Pearl River in Guangdong province in southern China. It differs from *Jiangnan Sizhu* in instrumentation. The melody line is very bright and lively due to the lead instrument, the gaohu—a higher-pitched two-string fiddle. (The gaohu is never used in *Jiangnan Sizhu* music.) Most of the melodies are based on local operas and folk tunes, mixed with melodies from central China. This *Guangdong* style is very young, originating in the 1920s, and much of the repertoire consists of new compositions. *Guangdong Yinyue* melodies are fast-paced and rhythmic, and some even have Western elements mixed in.

"Thunder in a Dry Season" is included in standard pipa repertoire for Level II exam requirements in China. The fingering is based on pipa master Lin Shicheng's score, but small changes here make it playable by a beginner. Some tips:

- As always, start slowly. Make sure the fast sixteenth notes are played evenly, and gradually increase your speed until you are comfortable with the techniques for both hands.

- You will need to make many fast position changes. Some of the passages include open strings to allow you time to move to the next position. Think ahead; your left hand should move to the next position while you are plucking the open string.

- "Thunder in a Dry Season" depicts the happiness and hopefulness of the Guangdong people as they hear thunder for the first time in many days after enduring a long drought. Your playing should be lively and spirited to express this happy feeling.

THUNDER IN A DRY SEASON 旱天雷

♩ = 118   Open-String Tuning 1=D (5 1 2 5)   Guangdong Music 廣東音樂

VIDEOS 74–76
(left hand/right hand/both)

80

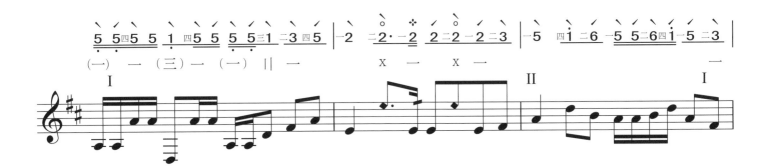

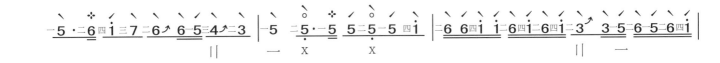

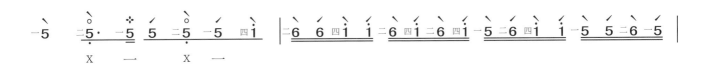

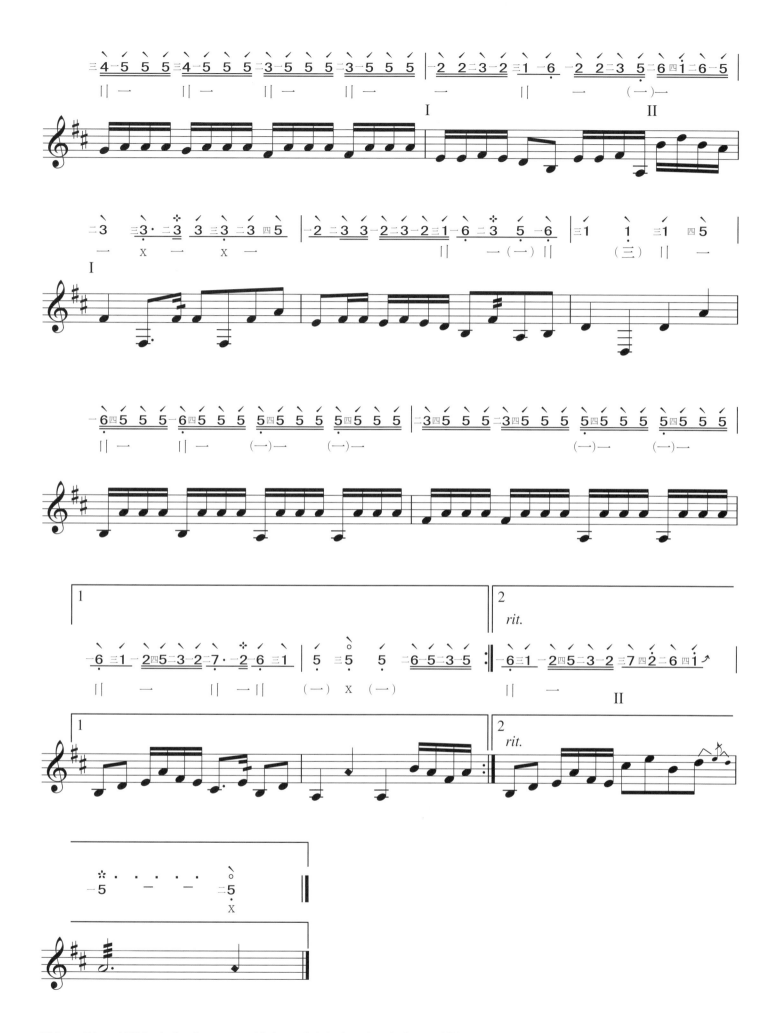

Videos 74 and 75 include close-ups of left- and right-hand techniques; Video 76 shows both hands playing the entire piece at full speed.

CLASSICAL PIPA REPERTOIRE

"White Snow in Sunny Spring" (Yang Chun Bai Xue) is also called "Sunny Spring Old Tune" (Yang Chun Gu Qu). It's one of the most popular classical pieces in the *Wen*-style repertoire. There are many versions, and one from each pipa school—*Pudong*, *Pinghu*, *Chongming*, and *Wang*. The following version is from the *Wang* School. It is included in the Standard Pipa Level III Exam Requirement repertoire, and is the most played version in China today. The score is based on *Wang* school pipa master Wei Zhongle's performance, and was transcribed by his two students, Qiu Chunyao and Ye Xuran.

The main melody is based on the Silk and Bamboo *Jiangnan Sizhu* folk tune "Old Six Beats." There are seven sections, each featuring variations (*Jia Hua*). Fresh and lively melodies played at a fast pace vividly describe the transition from winter to spring, and the reawakening of all things prosperous. The music evokes the infinite vitality of spring that gives such happiness and excitement to the people.

"White Snow in Sunny Spring" is a masterpiece, but it can also be used for training at many different levels. Since it has a lot of basic left-hand and right-hand techniques such as *Lun*, *Tui*, *La*, *Fanyin*, *Sao*, and *Fo*, it's perfect for beginners to practice their techniques while enjoying one of the most popular and elegant classical pieces for pipa.

Videos 77–90 are slow demos of all seven sections on both left hand and right hand; Video 91 is the whole piece at the proper tempo. Learn each section one by one; do not try to play them all right away. Start at a slow tempo, and gradually speed up after you are comfortable with all the techniques for both hands.

Notes:

① Use *Shang Tui* ↗ (上推) "push" technique. For the rest of the bends, *La* "pull" technique should be used. For all sections that repeat the same passages, the techniques would be the same.

② (*Gou* (勾): The right-hand thumbnail tip plucks the string towards the left side. It's like *Zhe* ( ) without the first finger.

③ ↘⁙ ▪   ▪   ▪   ▪   ▪ *Sao Lun* (掃輪): *Sao* followed by many five-finger tremolos in a row, played without stopping between the two techniques. It's similar to five-finger *Lun*'s index finger playing *Sao* instead of *Tan*. The index finger only plays *Sao* ↘ once, then the middle finger starts the tremolos. Do not play *Tan* again after *Sao*.

④ ╱⁙ ▪   ▪   ▪   ▪   ▪ *Tiao Lun* (挑輪): Combined with *Tiao* are many five-finger tremolos in a row without stopping between the techniques.

You can play the *Sao Lun* and *Tiao Lun* passages like this:

1) start with *Sao*, then play the first four-finger *Lun* (starting with the middle finger);

2) continue with the second four-finger *Lun*, then *Tiao* second string;

3) continue with four-finger *Lun*, then five-finger *Lun* starting with the thumb.

If there were marks for every finger, it would look like this:

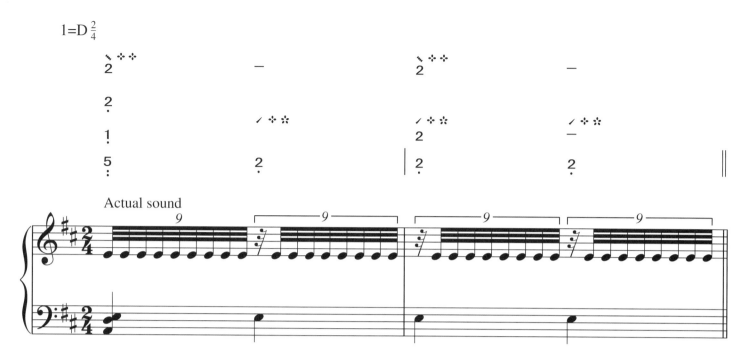

WHITE SNOW IN SUNNY SPRING (YANG CHUN BAI XUE) 陽春白雪

VIDEOS 77–78
(left hand/right hand)

Section 1: Best of All (Du Zhan Ao Tou) 獨占鰲頭

♩ = 100   Open-String Tuning 1=D (5 1 2 5)

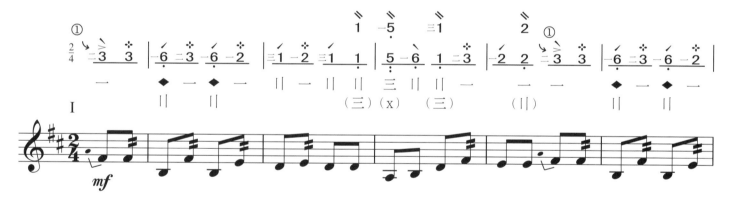

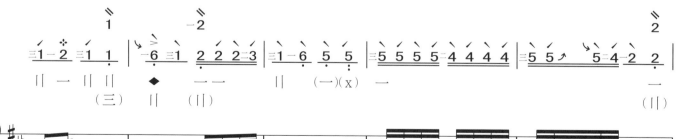

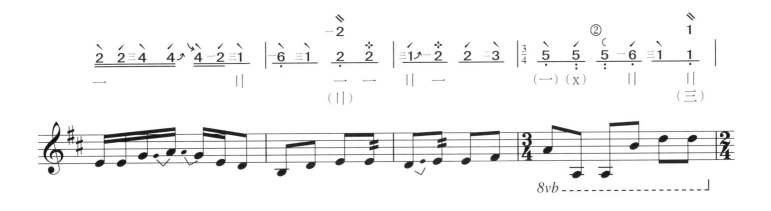

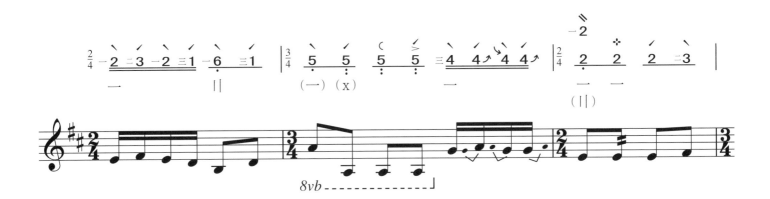

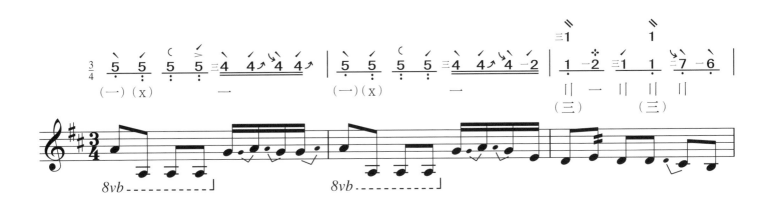

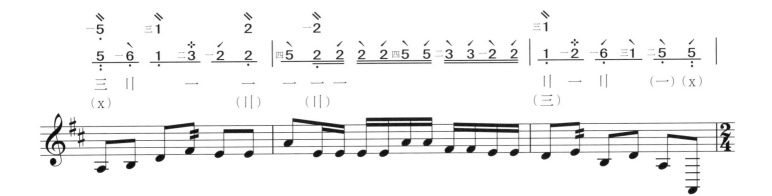

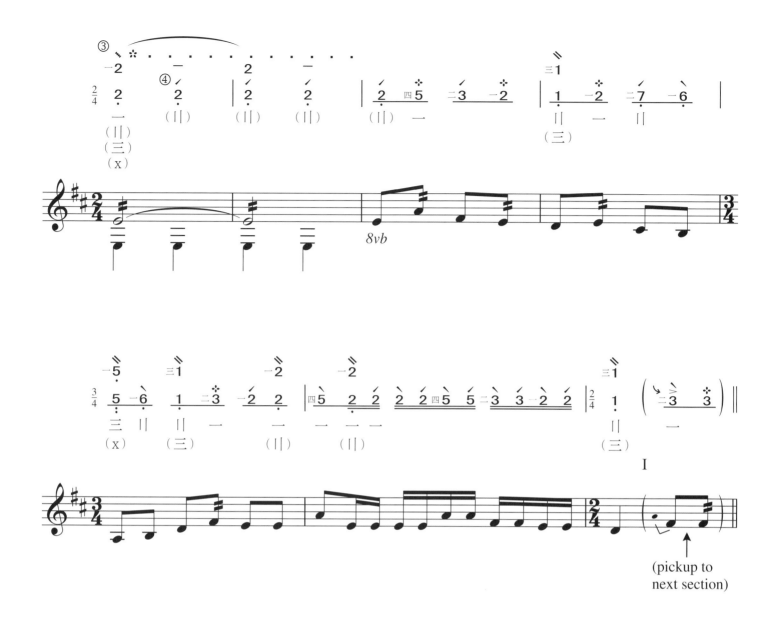

HOLIDAYS AND FOOD IN CHINA, PART 1

In China, many of the traditional holidays are associated with eating particular foods and dishes. The foods were chosen for either their visual or aural resemblance to important traditional things in Chinese culture. Chinese people believe eating good food helps bring them good luck, health, and prosperity, and brings family and friends together.

Chun Jie (春節)—Chinese New Year or "Spring Festival." (Chun means "Spring;" Jie means "Festival.") Chun Jie starts the first day of the lunar calendar. Each year the beginning date will differ, though it most often occurs in late January or early February. The celebration lasts 15 days. The most famous foods related to Chun Jie are:

- **Jiaozi** (餃子)—Chinese dumplings: these dumplings look like ancient money, so it is believed that eating a lot of jiaozi on New Year's Eve or New Year's Day can bring a person lots of money in the coming year.

- **Niangao** (年糕)—sticky rice cake: Nian means "year;" Gao means "cake," and also means "high." During the Chinese New Year, Niangao is eaten to make the new year better (higher). It's the same pronunciation as 年高.

VIDEOS 79–80
(left hand/right hand)

♩ = 130   Open-String Tuning 1=D (5̣ 1 2 5̇)

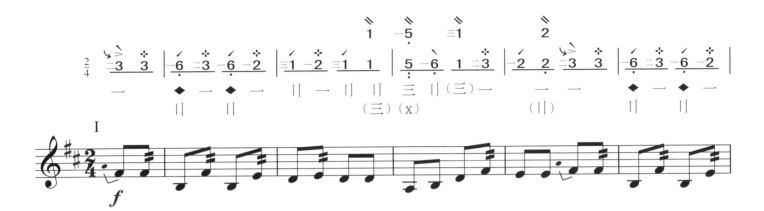

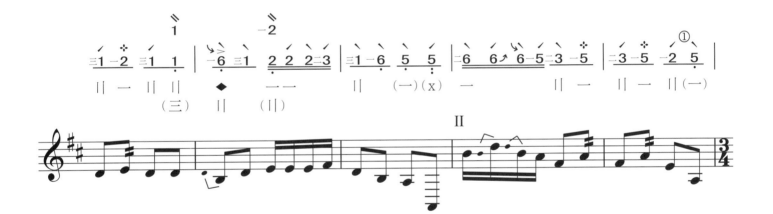

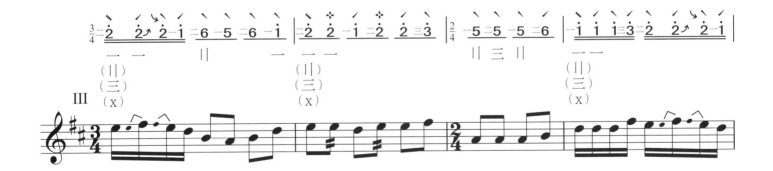

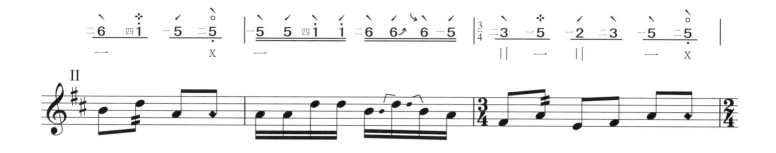

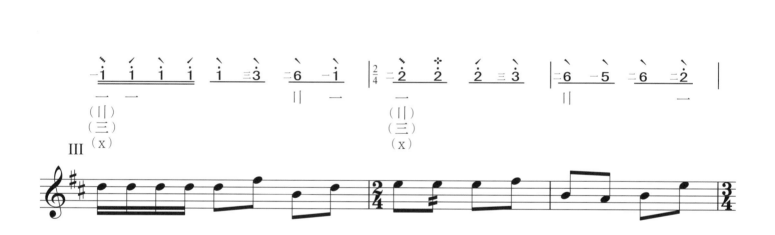

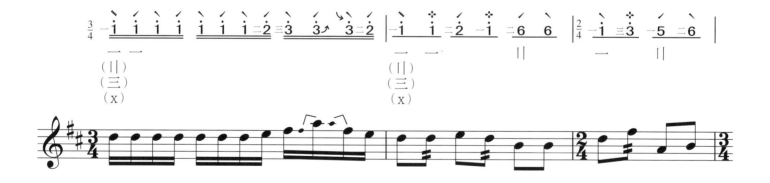

88

① This is the "using an open string to change position" technique. While plucking the open string, the left hand needs to move to the third position simultaneously. Do not wait until after you pluck the open string to move to the next position.

"White Snow in Sunny Spring" Section 3: Bright Moon (Yi Lun Ming Yue) 一輪明月

VIDEOS 81–82
(left hand/right hand)

♩ = 130　　　Open-String Tuning 1=D (5 1 2 5)

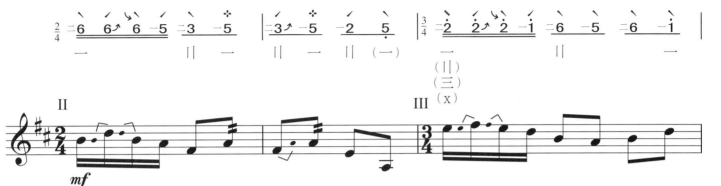

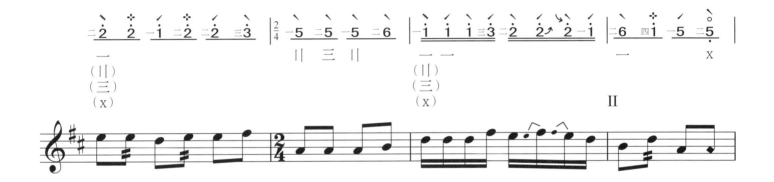

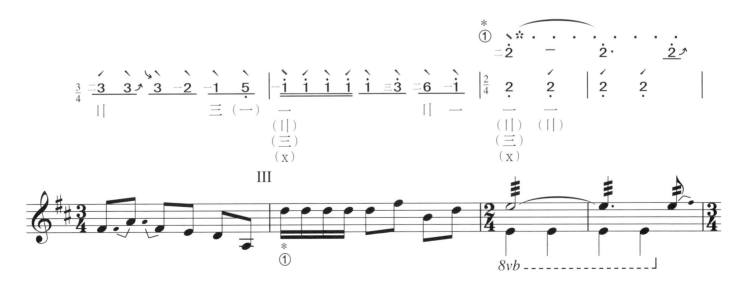

* ① Please play this [symbol] . . . . . *Sao Lun* (掃輪) and [symbol] . . . . . *Tiao Lun* (挑輪) passage as taught on page 83.

HOLIDAYS AND FOOD IN CHINA, PART 2

Like Chinese New Year, these other important Chinese holidays have specific foods associated with them.

Yaun Xiao Jie (元宵節)—Lantern Festival: On the 15th day of the first lunar month, the New Year's celebration concludes with the Lantern Festival. The food that must be eaten on the day of the Lantern Festival is Yuan Xiao (元宵) or Tang Yuan (湯圓): sticky rice balls boiled in water. Yuan Xiao or Tang Yuan alludes to Tuan Yuan (團圓), which symbolizes unity and a peaceful family.

Zhong Qiu Jie (中秋節)—Mid-Autumn Festival or Moon Festival: This occurs on the 15th day of the eighth month in the lunar calendar—between mid-September and early October. The most famous food eaten on this day is Yuebing (月餅) or "moon cake," consisting mainly of a sweet or savory filling baked in crust. The round shape resembles a full moon. While people eat moon cake they also enjoy the glorious full moon. This festival has become a very important family event for Chinese, similar to Thanksgiving in America. It is also called Tuan Yuan Jie (團圓節), "Family Gathering Together Festival." Even if you and your loved ones are not in the same location and are not eating together, since you are sharing the same full moon in the sky it feels like you are still under the same roof. That's why it is called the "Moon Festival"; it's a reunion of families or sending of thoughts from afar as they rejoice together in thought while eating moon cake and gazing at the moon.

♩ = 130   Open-String Tuning 1=D (5̣ 1 2 5)

VIDEOS 83–84
(left hand/right hand)

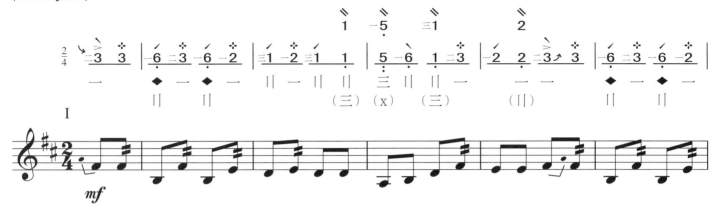

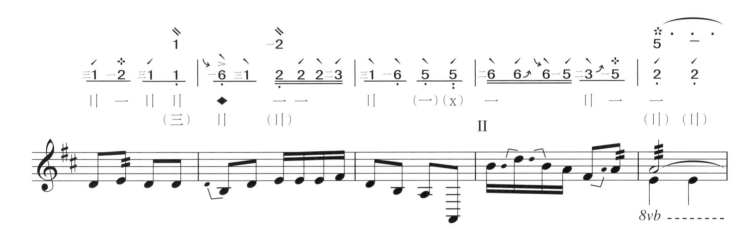

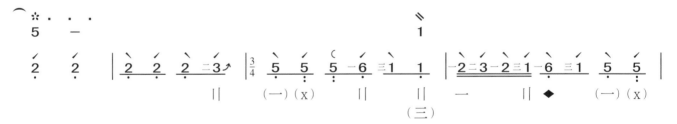

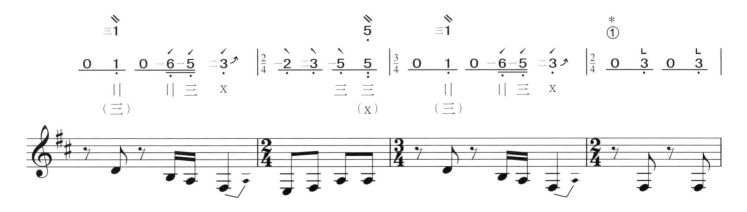

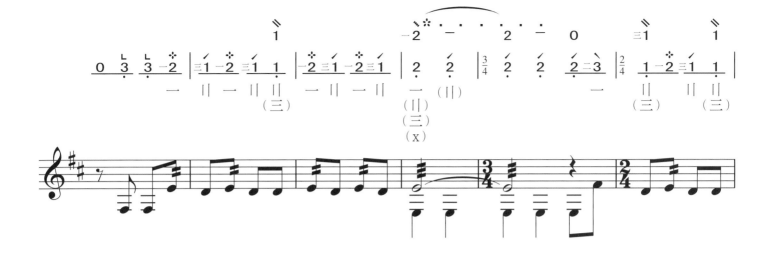

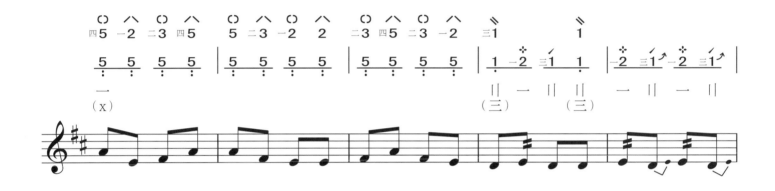

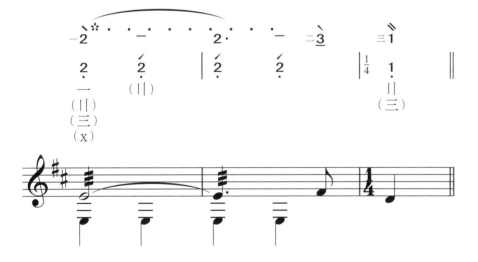

*① Make sure to rest for the right amount of time. After playing the *Pai* **L** on the fourth string, the next half *Lun* ⁘ needs to be connected smoothly. Do not slow down the tempo.

"White Snow in Sunny Spring" Section 5: Sounds from the Iron Stick (Tie Ban Ban Sheng) 鐵策板聲

VIDEOS 85–86
(left hand/right hand)

♩ = 130   Open-String Tuning 1=D (5 1 2 5)

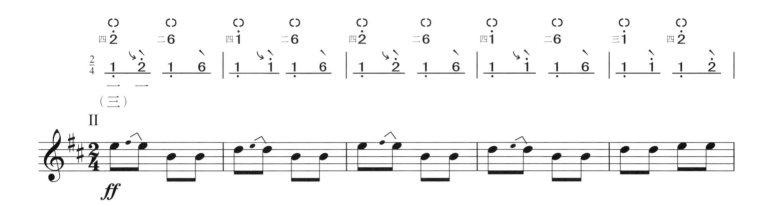

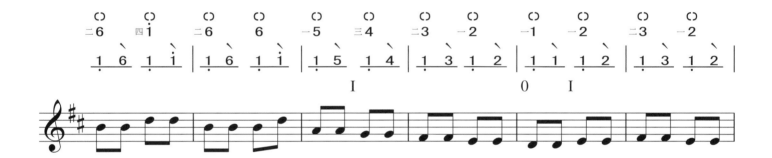

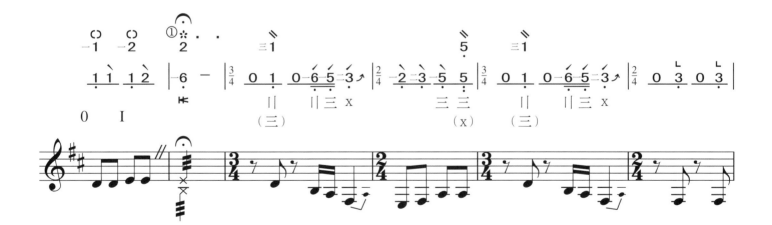

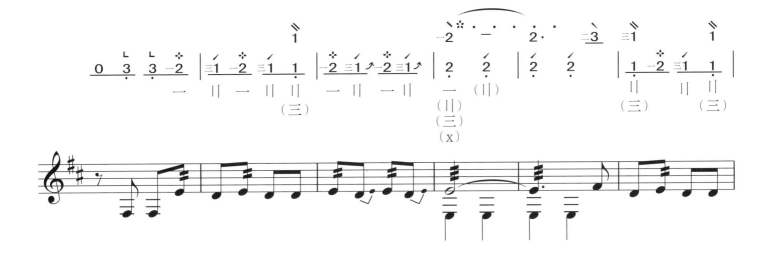

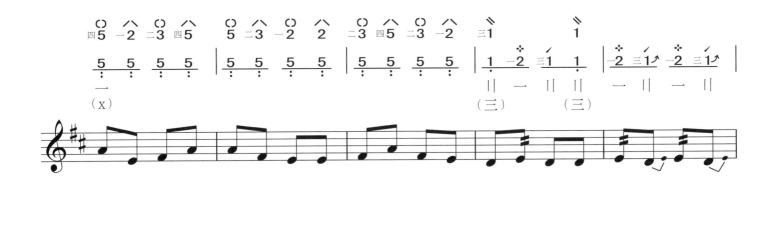

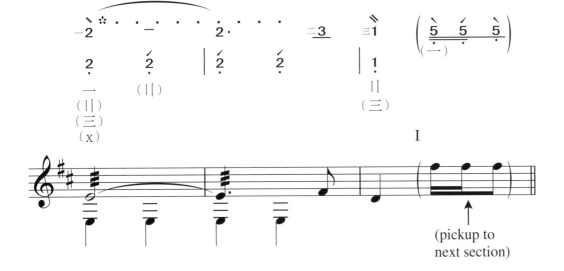

(pickup to
next section)

*① When playing *Jiao Xian*, use your ring finger to push the first string under the second string, then use your index finger to cross and press both strings.

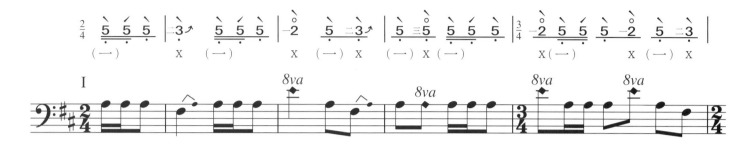

♩ = 130   Open-String Tuning 1=D (5̣ 1 2̇ 5̇)

VIDEOS 87–88
(left hand/right hand)

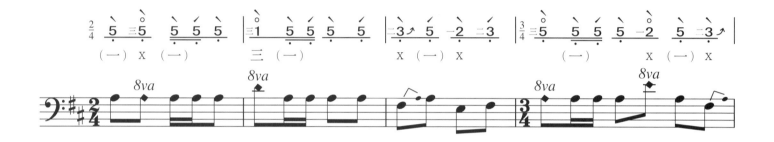

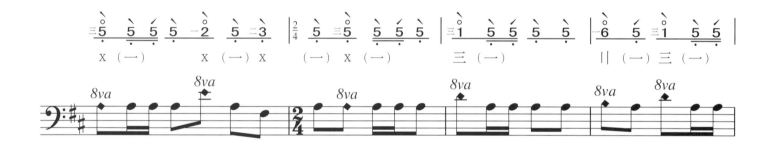

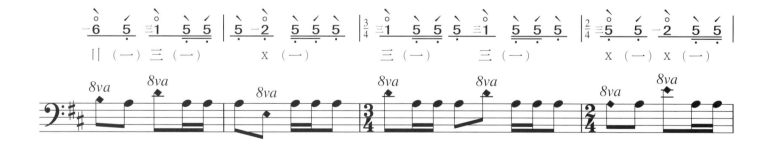

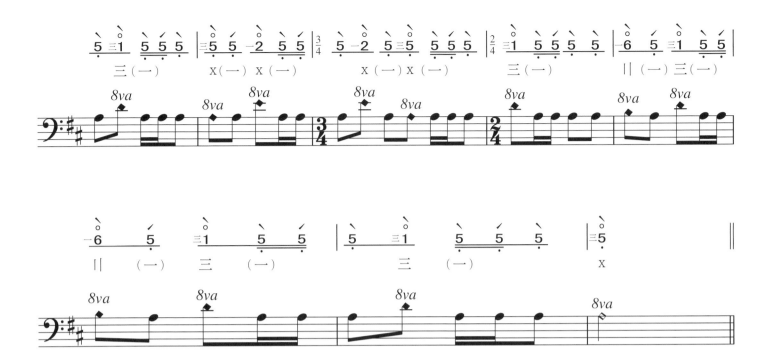

"White Snow in Sunny Spring" Section 7: Sounds of Cranes from the East Lake (Dong Gao He Ming) 東皋鶴鳴

VIDEOS 89–90
(left hand/right hand)

♩ = 150   Open-String Tuning 1=D (5̣ 1̣ 2̣ 5̣)

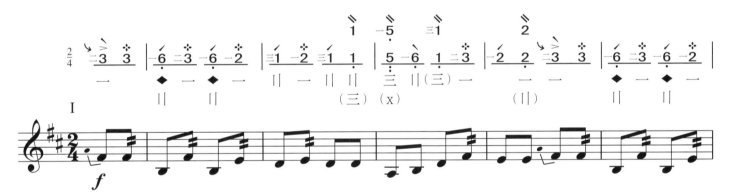

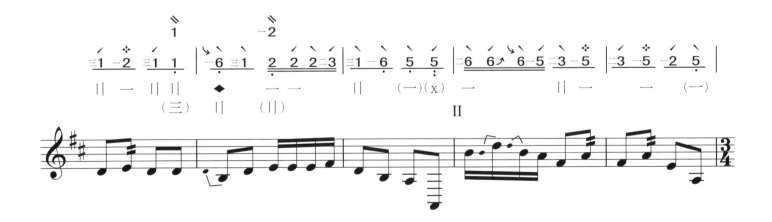

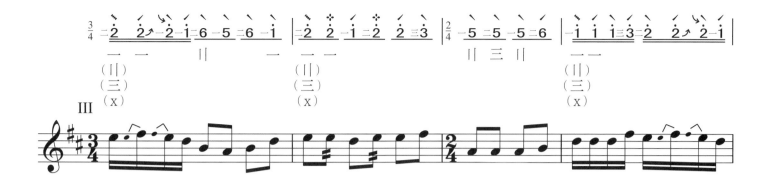

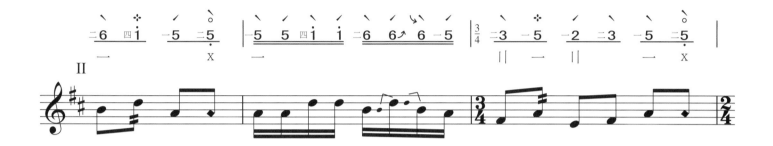

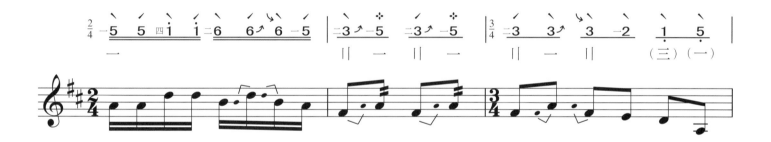

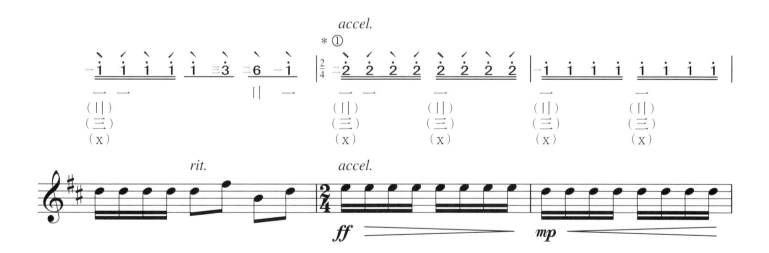

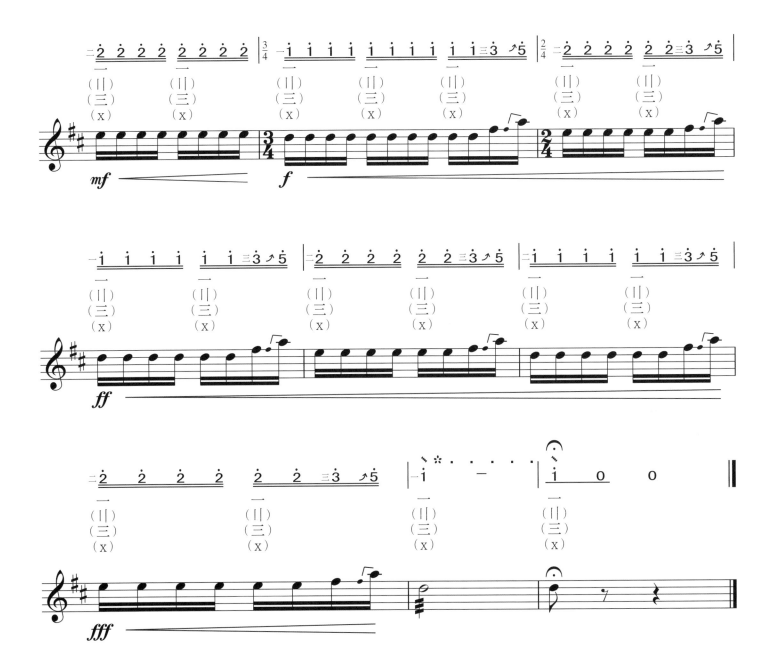

*① *Sao Jia Tan* ✷✎✎✎ (掃夾彈): Combines *Sao*, *Tiao*, *Tan*, and *Tao* in fast tempo without stopping between the techniques.

Start at a slow pace until your hand can play at a faster pace comfortably. Play these four notes as a group. Since the rest of the measures continue to use this same technique, it's not necessary to notate all technique marks on the subsequent notes.

And here is a full performance of all seven sections of "White Snow in Sunny Spring."

VIDEO 91

APPENDIX

COMPOSING FOR PIPA

In recent years, many composers worldwide have combined traditional Chinese instruments with Western instrumentation in their compositions. The pipa has been one of the most popular choices and is widely used in this fashion. Today there are numerous concerti for pipa and symphony orchestra as well as chamber pieces where the pipa plays a prominent role. Since I arrived in the United States over 20 years ago, I have worked with many composers. The most common request I receive from these composers is to provide resources that would allow them to learn how to best compose for pipa. I would like to offer some insights from my perspective as both a pipa player and composer.

- The best role for the pipa in any composition is to play melody lines. You can compose for the pipa as you would for violin or voice, and can use a variety of tremolos (such as *Lun*, *Gun*, etc.) to sustain long notes.

- The best ranges for melody lines fall in the first, second, and third positions.

- If you need to use chords, it is best to use ones that contain open strings, using techniques such as *Shuang Tan*, *Shuang Tiao*, *Sao*, *Fo*, *Zhe*, and *Fen*. It is difficult and awkward to play chords that contain three or more notes within the same octave; the use of open strings will ease this difficulty. If your composition requires a lot of chords that don't include open strings in the common tuning of A–D–E–A, you can alter the tuning of the strings if needed to accommodate your music. This is not a common procedure, but it is a very effective way to meet your needs.

- The most suitable keys for the pipa are D, G, C, F, or A. The most difficult keys to play in (due to the lack of open-string notes) are E♭, B♭, etc.

- Try to use as many left-hand techniques as possible, as this showcases sounds that are unique to the pipa and not available on other instruments. For example, a note can be bent up as far as a perfect 4th, and there are many different varieties of note-bending techniques and other left-hand techniques available on the pipa.

- Try to use as many of the special sound effects as are appropriate for your composition. These also showcase the uniqueness of the pipa. The following legends of sound effects and other technique symbols are for composers as well as pipa players.

These are just a few thoughts. Pipa players are always looking for wonderful compositions to add to their repertoire. Good luck with your creative compositions, and have fun!

PIPA SOUND EFFECTS

VIDEO 92

Here is a list of sound effects with cross-references to the appropriate chapters.

Sound Effects	Right-Hand Techniques	Left-Hand Techniques	Chapter(s)
Flowing Water	*Gua* (挂) ↟, *Lin*: (臨) ↡	*Fanyin* 泛音 O	Vibrato and Overtones Right-Hand Sound Effects
Bubbling Water	*Gua* (挂) ↟, *Lin*: (臨) ↡	Entire left hand touches strings while sliding up and down	Right-Hand Sound Effect Techniques
Blowing Wind	*Chang Lun* 長輪 ⁑ ▪ ▪ ▪ ▪ ▪	Left-hand finger slides up and down on the string	Tremolo / *Lun Zhi*
Chinese Gongs and Percussion		Jiao (絞) ⊢⊦	Left-Hand Special Techniques
Conversing Geese		*Shang La/Wan* (上拉 / 挽) ↗	Basic Left-Hand Techniques Part 1
Horses Trotting		*Zhai* (摘) ⅄	Right-Hand Sound Effect Techniques
Clashing Swords		*Sha* (煞) ⊥	Left-Hand Special Techniques
Cannon Shots	*Pai* (拍) ∟		Right-Hand Sound Effect Techniques
Fireworks	*Tan Mianban* (彈面板) ⊢		Right-Hand Sound Effect Techniques
People Talking in Chinese		*Le* (勒弦)	Advanced level, rarely used
People Laughing		*Le* (勒弦)	Advanced level, rarely used

STRING SYMBOLS

⼀	First String	(⼀)	First Open String
⏐⏐	Second String	(⏐⏐)	Second Open String
⼆	Third String	(⼆)	Third Open String
X	Fourth String	(X)	Fourth Open String

All string number symbols are placed under the note.

LEFT-HAND FINGERING SYMBOLS

一	Index Finger
二	Middle Finger
三	Ring Finger
四	Pinky
♂	Thumb

All fingering number marks are placed to the left of the note.

LEFT-HAND POSITION SYMBOLS

0	Xiang Position
I	First Position
II	Second Position
III	Third Position
X	Fourth Position

All position number marks are placed under the note.

LEFT-HAND TECHNIQUES

Technique Symbols	Name and Description
◆	*Yin* 吟: The left-hand finger presses the string near a fret and swings evenly from left to right.
▲	*Da* 打: Only a left-hand finger is used to hit the string on the note to produce a soft sound. (The right hand is not used.)
'	*Sou* 擞: Only a left-hand finger is used to pluck the string on the note to produce a soft sound. (The right hand is not used.)
⌣	*Dai* 带: After a right-hand finger plucks the string and the left-hand finger presses the string, the left-hand finger is lifted off the note quickly to produce a soft sound.
↗	*Shang La/Tui* 上拉 / 推: Pull / The string is pushed from a lower pitch to a higher pitch, then released back to the original pitch.
↘	*Xia La/Tui* 上拉 / 推: Pull / The string is pushed to a higher pitch first, then plucked while being released allowing it to fall back to the original pitch.

扏	*Jiao* 絞: The left-hand ring finger pushes the first string under the second string, then pulls the second string to cross over the top of the first string.
○	*Fanyin* 泛音: The left-hand finger(s) barely touch the string directly above the fret(s) while the right-hand finger simultaneously plucks the string(s).
⑅	*Fu* 伏: The left-hand or right-hand fingers cover the string, stopping the sound suddenly.
⊥	*Sha* 煞: A left-hand fingernail is placed under the string and presses against the string to produce a percussive sound.

All left-hand symbols are placed above the note.

Exceptions: ◆ 扏 ⑅ marks are placed under the notes and ↘ marks are placed adjacent to the note.

RIGHT-HAND TECHNIQUES

Technique Symbols	Name and the Description
＼	*Tan* 彈: The index finger plucks the string with a downward motion.
／	*Tiao* 挑: The thumb plucks the string with an upward motion.
＼＼	*Shuang Tan* 雙彈: The index finger plucks with a downward motion on two strings.
／／	*Shuang Tiao* 雙挑: The thumb plucks with an upward motion on two strings.
⊂⊃	*Zhe* 摭:The index finger and thumb pluck the two outer strings simultaneously with the fingernail tip and thumbnail tip moving towards each other.
∧	*Fen* 分: The index finger and thumb pluck the two outer strings simultaneously with the fingernail tip and thumbnail tip moving in opposite directions.
⸫	*San Zhi Lun* 三指輪: Three-Finger Tremolo. *Tan* and *Tiao*, and then adding the middle finger, *Ti*, in between.
⸬	*Si Zhi Lun* 四指輪 / 半輪: Four-Finger Tremolo or Half Tremolo. The index finger, middle finger, ring finger, and pinky pluck the string with a downward motion.
⁙	*Wu Zhi Lun/Quan Lun* 五指輪/全輪: Five-Finger Tremolo or Whole Tremolo. The index finger, middle finger, ring finger, and pinky pluck the string with a downward motion and the thumb plucks the string with an upward motion.
⸜	*Sao* 掃: The index finger strikes with a downward motion on four strings.
⸝	*Fo* 佛: The thumb strikes with an upward motion on four strings.
／／／	*Gun* 滾: *Tan* and *Tiao* at fast tempo and a combination of several *Gun Zhi* in a row without stopping.
⁙ ▪ ▪ ▪ ▪	*Chang Lun* 長輪: Combining many five-finger tremolos in a row without stopping, resulting in one long tremolo.

↖	*Ti* 剔: The middle finger plucks the string with a downward motion.
(	*Gou* 勾: The thumbnail tip plucks the string toward the left.
↖⁑ · · · ·	*Sao Lun* 掃輪: Combines *Tiao* and many five-finger tremolos in a row without stopping between the two techniques.
╱⁑ · · · ·	*Tiao Lun* 挑輪: Combines *Sao* and many five-finger tremolos in a row without stopping between the two techniques.
↖╱↘╱	*Sao Jia Tan* 掃夾彈: Combines *Sao* with *Tiao*, *Tan*, and *Tao* at a fast tempo without stopping between the techniques. Notes are played as a group.
⬆	*Gua/Hua* 挂/划: The index finger plucks from fourth string to first string with a downward motion.
⬇	*Lin* 臨: The thumb plucks from first string to fourth string with an upward motion.
⅄	*Zhai* 摘: The thumbnail presses on the string, and the index or middle finger plucks the string at the same time to produce a bright, percussive sound.
∟	*Pai* 拍: The thumb pulls up on the fourth string quickly and loudly to produce a loud slapping sound. (Only used on the fourth string.)
⻊	*Ti* 提: The thumb and index finger hold one string together, lift it up, and slap it back quickly and loudly to produce a surprising, explosive sound.
⊢	*Tan Mianban* 彈面板: The index and/or middle fingernails are used to strike the wood on the lower part of the pipa belly to produce a bright popping sound.

All right-hand symbols are placed on the top of the note.

Exceptions: ⬆ and ⬇ are placed on the left side of the note.